THOUGHT AND ACTION

THOUGHT
AND ACTION

By

Stuart Hampshire

Fellow of All Souls College, Oxford

1965

CHATTO AND WINDUS

LONDON

Published By
Chatto and Windus Ltd
42 William IV Street
London WC 2

★

Clarke. Irwin and Co Ltd
Toronto

First Published July 1959
Second Impression January 1960
Third Impression August 1965

PRINTED PHOTOLITHO IN GREAT BRITAIN
BY EBENEZER BAYLIS AND SON, LTD.
THE TRINITY PRESS, WORCESTER, AND LONDON

To Renee

CONTENTS

INTRODUCTION

THIS essay revolves around certain familiar contrasts: the contrast between that which is unavoidable in the structure of human thought and that which is contingent and changeable: between inner thought and its natural expression in speech and action: between that which confronts a man as the situation before him and that which is his own response to it: between knowledge and decision: between criticism and practice: between abstract philosophical opinions and the concrete varieties of experience. I did not hope to find definite solutions to the problems connected with these contrasts. I hoped to trace connections between these contrasts, connections that are now often overlooked, and to bring moral argument nearer to the philosophy of mind, and the philosophy of mind nearer to moral argument. In philosophy, as in other inquiries, it has been the discipline of this time to answer separable questions separately, to analyse complex difficulties into elementary difficulties. The rewards of this discipline have been very great: accuracy, clarity, and sometimes even conclusiveness. But it is possible that there are purposes and interests which require that accurate and step-by-step analysis should not always be preferred to a more general survey and more tentative opinions, even in philosophy. It is possible that some moral and political interests, which, if pressed far enough, certainly lead into philosophy, are of this character: that they require more general statements of opinion, a summary of a

9

philosophical position, in addition to the detailed analysis of particular problems.

I wish to acknowledge my debt to Professor H. L. A. Hart, who read the book in manuscript and made valuable suggestions and corrected mistakes, and to Mr D. F. Pears.

Chapter 1

PERSONS AND THEIR SITUATION

MEN may think with a view to knowledge, or they may think with a view to action. They may ask themselves 'Is this statement true or is it not?' and also 'Shall I do this or shall I not?' Both kinds of question can be formulated in words, and there would be nothing properly called thought unless such questions could be formulated in words. Words are by definition parts of a language. A language is, among other things, a set of signs actually used by intelligent beings to refer to recurrent elements in their experience and in reality. Men may use language to refer to recurrent elements in their experience and in reality for many different purposes. They may refer to something in order to give some information about it, to make a request about it, to give an order about it, to give a promise about it, to express admiration of it, and for countless other purposes which are distinguishable as different forms of human behaviour and as different social institutions. Whatever the purposes for which a language is used, a language is always a means of singling out, and directing attention to, certain elements of experience and reality as subjects which can be referred to again and again. A language must provide a means of differentiating, of dividing, reality into the pieces and segments which are to be constant subjects of reference. Reality and experience cannot be thought about unless we have rules that correlate particular groups of signs with particular recurrent elements in reality and experience, in such a way that any familiar use of a particular group of signs will be taken as a reference to some particular element in experience.

These rules are necessarily of two related types: first, rules that single out elements in reality as being of the same kind, and that identify recurring kinds of thing: secondly, rules that single out one specimen of a certain kind from another, and that identify the same one as recurring or appearing again. Rules of the first type may be called principles of classification: rules of the second type may be called principles of individuation. Rules of the two types are systematically connected.

When we use a language in our own thought and in communication with others, we are so far accepting that particular division of reality into segments which the vocabulary and grammar of that particular language impose. It seems that we can set no theoretical limit to the number of different ways in which reality could be divided into recurrent elements for the purposes of thought and action; for there is no sense in 'could' or 'could not' as they are used here, unless we have first given the rules or principles that would exclude certain methods of differentiation as impossible. But to give such rules or principles for singling out and differentiating elements in reality is precisely to explain the structure of a possible or actual language. In order to show that elements in reality *could* only be distinguished for the purposes of language in one familiar way, we would have to show that nothing else would count as 'distinguishing elements in reality for the purposes of language'. We would have to establish some restrictive definition either of 'referring to reality' or of 'language', or of both. Such a definition need not be a trivial elucidation of a word, and it has certainly been a large part of philosophy to try to achieve it, or to approach towards it. Anyone who has tried to state—and all philosophers have tried—the relation of man's thought and knowledge to reality has either tried to set some limits to what can be counted as 'reality', or to what can be counted as 'thought' or 'knowledge'. In the critical phase of philosophy, since Kant, it has been evident that there can be only one, and not two, questions here. This question is —what are the conditions necessary for making statements and for making any recognisable distinction between truth and falsity in referring to reality? In answering this question, one is driven to consider, in the most general terms possible, the principles of differentiation that must always be involved in correlating words, or other symbols, with elements of reality. Any actual language, and any system of thought within a language, taken at random as an example, will exhibit some characteristic variation of the most general principles of differentiation which, as far as we can see, are used in *every* application of language to reality. But we cannot then say with absolute finality that these most general principles of differentiating elements in reality are the only possible ones; this would be the error of Kant, the belief that we can anticipate and set final limits to new forms of knowledge. The institutions of language are always developing, and the history of their development is the history of the human mind. Even less can we suppose that there must be some independently identifiable ground in reality, independent of the conditions of reference to reality, for the manner in which we differentiate elements in reality; this would be the error of the pre-critical metaphysicians before Kant. We cannot give a sense to this opposition between the nature of reality and the conditions of our knowledge of it. We can call our most general principles of singling out and differentiating, elements in reality 'necessities of discourse', or 'necessary presuppositions of thought and knowledge', as a way of saying that we cannot either explain or justify these principles by reference to any principles that are still more general in their application. 'Necessary' here means no more than 'ultimate' in the sense of 'most general' and therefore 'not to be further explained'. The implication of 'necessary' is not that there are statable alternatives that for some further reason are impossible; rather that we cannot so far conceive, and formulate, any alternative principles of differentiation, which are not specimens of this most general type. But we can explain and justify our use of any one particular system of thought, or of language, or of part of a language, as involving variations of those most general principles of differentiating elements in reality that we find in all types of discourse. We may look for the point or purpose of these variations, and we may make comparisons between them. We may explain why one type of discourse involves discriminating elements in reality on a particular principle that would be out of place in another type of discourse serving a largely different need. We have to explain the types of discourse by reference to the institutions and forms of social life with which they are associated. This notion of different types of discourse is always recognised and used, even outside philosophy. Philosophers, beginning with Aristotle, have tried to draw the many possible dividing lines more precisely and in accordance with some very general principles.

The principle of division must be found in some relation between the manner in which subject-terms are singled out and the purposes which these varying methods of identification are intended to serve. The units, or elements of reality, singled out for the purposes of physical science are, in virtue of the method of identification, different in type from the elements that we single out for the purposes of ordinary communication about physical things. We may fall into error, and be confused, if we do not understand the point or purpose of these differences, and if we suppose that reality must be properly represented as wholly consisting either of one type of element or of the other. Equally we cannot suppose that there is an abrupt and clear discontinuity between the elements of two different types, or between the methods by which we distinguish them. The two types of element may be referred to in a single argument and in a single sentence, and relations may be stated between these things or units of different types. Although the principles of differentiation applied to the particles of physics are very different from the principles by which we single out familiar physical things as objects of reference, there is a range of intermediate cases between these two extremes. We cannot make a simple and absolute separation between different levels of language. They have all been developed in the same context of a common social life.

Any application of language and thought to reality involves the differentiation of elements in reality as objects of reference, which is to say that it involves giving sense to expressions of the form 'a so-and-so'. One must be in a position to use an expression which has the force, or plays the part of, 'That is a so-and-so'. This is only the truism that, if I am to speak about anything, I must have the means of referring to something in particular. To give a sense to any expression which replaces 'so-and-so' is to give instructions for distinguishing 'so-and-so's' from anything else: not only to give the means of recognising so-and-so's in general, but also to state what makes any so-and-so the same so-and-so. I must have a means of deciding whether the same thing is still being referred to or whether the topic has changed. There would otherwise be no means of contradicting the statement made, and therefore no distinction between truth and falsity. There may be identifiable objects of reference—for example, flashes of lightning or peals of thunder or clouds—in respect of which we scarcely make the distinction between one so-and-so and another. There are many identifiable objects of reference for which we do not require any exact principle of individuation, in the sense of a principle of counting, that is, the means of distinguishing between one, two and three so-and-so's. But we always need to attach a sense to 'the same so-and-so', where the same so-and-so can be a constant object of reference in a succession of statements, that is, we always need some criterion of identity, however rough and indeterminate it may be. It is unavoidable that the thinking subject should need to think and speak about the same thing at different times, the thinking subject being liable to change and the object under reference also being liable to change. Not all kinds of objects singled out in reality in fact persist for any length of time. But it must always make sense to ask how long the object referred to existed and to inquire into its history, whatever kind of thing it is. The singling out, or identification, of something as a so-and-so, which involves the correlation of an expression with something in reality, is always the application of a rule that determines the meaning of the expression. The rule is a rule of identity, in the sense that it prescribes the conditions not only of distinguishing so-and-so's from any other kinds of thing, which are in other respects like them, but also of distinguishing 'the same so-and-so' throughout its history as a constant individual object of reference. And this is not a necessity merely in the grammar of a few languages; it is a necessity in any language whatever in which statements are to be made and contradicted.

Singling out elements in reality as constant objects of reference is singling out persisting things. I am in effect arguing that we must unavoidably think of reality as consisting of persisting things of different types and kinds. One may ask why reality must be conceived as consisting of things of different types and kinds rather than of events or processes of different types and kinds. The necessity so far mentioned is only that there should be a type of term which enters into utterances having the function of 'This is a so-and-so'. Whether the so-and-so that is identified is to be called a thing rather than a process is a question that can only be answered in the context of a particular grammar that already distinguishes nouns and verbs in a particular way. The necessity of conceiving reality as consisting of things is only the necessity of finding some persisting and recurrent objects of reference, when the reference is made by a person occupying a particular position and speaking from this standpoint. No more specific sense is here attached to the type-word 'thing'. One might try to imagine a language in which shades of colour were singled out as objects of reference; and certainly we can and do refer to shades of colour by their names. But we cannot ask for the history of this same shade of colour, if this includes asking how it (the shade of colour) came to be here, to be pointed at by the speaker, at this time. If we try to ask this question, we find ourselves asking for the history of this *patch* of colour. Then the patch of colour becomes, in the sense required, a kind of thing. In order to communicate, we need to have the means of referring to elements in reality which have a history, that tells how they came to be here, standing in this relation to this speaker as objects of reference. If we had no means of making such references, we would never be able to pick out, to pinpoint, any particular place and time, any particular situation, as the object of our reference. As reality is always changing, and more important, as we are also constantly changing our standpoint, we need points of reference, or attachment, which are identifiably the same through change. Without these points of attachment, all our statements would be unrestricted general statements, unrelated to reality by any indication of particular segments of reality; and this is a self-contradictory hypothesis. There seems therefore no conceivable alternative, in any language fit for statement-making, to some distinction that roughly corresponds to the distinction between a thing and its changing properties, however various the types of thing singled out may be. Even if I try to suppose myself confined for the whole of my life in a space where everything perceptible was a fluid of the same colour, or where everything was made of quicksilver, I would still be driven to single out some more or less persistent configurations as objects of reference, if I wanted to make any statements at all. And the supposition can scarcely be made, if I try to retain the thought of myself as the stable observer of this fluid or quicksilver world.

An identification, or singling out, of a particular element in reality is expressible in some formula that has the force of 'This is a so-and-so'. This formula can only be effective in communication if it is always possible to give some answer to the question 'What is?' i.e. 'What are you referring to by "this"?' We need to know what is being identified as what. From this necessity alone two general truths can be deduced, truths that can also be established by other arguments. First, an identification of some element

18

in reality as a so-and-so is intelligible only as one of a whole system of possible identifications, that is, if there is a language in being. Secondly, any element in reality identified as a so-and-so may always be classified in an indefinite number of alternative ways. This second conclusion needs elaboration, because it has large consequences. We may be inclined to think of the elements that we single out in reality as already singled out for us, each marked off as uniquely classifiable in a certain way. Or we may think that the same thing is marked off for us in reality as the same thing, independently of our already established methods of identifying particular kinds of thing. It may seem that the elements or units are already marked off for us as different things, but that in different languages, or in different systems of thought, different elements are noticed and that different names are given to the same elements. But when we consider that every identification of something as a so-and-so allows also that the same thing should also be classified as a thing of some other kind, it becomes evident that 'the same thing' can always be counted as two or more different things, if we once suppose ourselves to be counting just things, rather than things of a particular kind. The only possible conclusion is that we cannot count, or differentiate, different things simply as different things; we can only count things as things of a certain kind. Reality cannot be divided into so many—even infinitely many— different things in such a way that, in counting the different things that there are, I have some means of not counting 'the same thing' twice. In any particular case, when I am required to make an inventory of the things that there are, I can only avoid mentioning the same thing twice by adhering to a single system of classification, that is, by making my list a list of things of a certain kind. If I do not assume some single principle of classification, I cannot even begin my inventory. As soon as I say 'This is one thing and that is another', I must be in a position to say what things are referred to by 'This and that' in order to give sense to, and to pin down, my reference. In saying what things I am referring to I already make the differentiation between the two things, by saying 'the so-and-so' and 'the so-and-so'. I could also find some classification that would permit me to refer to the pair of things so differentiated together, and therefore as constituting a single thing; and I could also refer to some distinguishable part, aspect or element of each of them separately.

Whatever I may be referring to and identifying as a thing of a certain kind, I am always and necessarily amplifying the description that might originally be given of it: 'That heap of stones is a tomb'. Having established these two identifications, I can go on to a third identification of the same form and so on indefinitely. There is no necessary end to the series. Nor is there a necessary starting-point, as so many philosophers have assumed, in a type of classification which most nearly corresponds to the true divisions in experience or reality. It must depend on our permanent and common interests, and the forms of our social life, whether we tend to single out one or another type of object in our language as constant objects of reference. It depends on the form of civilisation, of which the language is a part, as one social institution among others. The institution of language presupposes a background of non-linguistic convention, the social world of conventionalised gesture, expression and habits of co-operation. However far we press the demand for an ultimate and natural object of reference, which is somehow unavoidable and obvious, we only arrive at a terminus, provided that we assume the common interests of persons, concrete objects among other objects, in their communication with each other. It is reasonably certain that in any natural language the objects of reference primitively chosen will be persisting things, differentiated into kinds, at least in part, by their usefulness in serving different, but constant, human needs. It is natural, but not strictly inevitable, that the principle of identification and differentiation of kinds of thing will generally be of the form 'usable for such-and-such a purpose', that is, anything that can be used to serve exactly the same human need will count as the same kind of thing, irrespective of other kinds of difference, for example, differences of appearance. It is virtually inconceivable that we should differentiate elements in reality principally by the criterion of their sensory properties alone, by their colour, shape, smell and taste. There is no easily imaginable condition of society in which we would communicate and calculate primarily as aesthetes, and therefore we are not principally interested in singling out constant configurations of sensory properties. Plainly the criteria by which we distinguish different types of thing in reality are complex and various, and no generalisation can be altogether valid. There is no theoretically determinable limit to the variety of new types of classification that may be introduced. There will be as many new types of classification as there will be new forms of social life and of co-operation among men.

From all these considerations a conclusion may be drawn in a single phrase: description of reality is essentially inexhaustible. It is in principle impossible that we should ever come to the end of it and complete our description. This is true, not only because we cannot set limits to reality or give a possible sense to the words 'I have identified all the things that there are'; but, more strongly, because we cannot even give sense to the words 'I have identified all the things that there are in this room'. The inexhaustibility lies in the nature of description and identification, however restricted they may be.

There are kinds of notation, and systems of symbols, which may serve as a contrast with language, as language is used to refer to reality, and which may help in explaining the essential indeterminateness of language. A record of a game of chess, a score-book in cricket, are in different ways, and to different degrees, determinate, first, in the sense that a more or less complete and exhaustive account of the game can be given within these notations, and, secondly, that this would be the only and the finally correct account of the game. The notation that describes a game can be in this sense determinate, because it is laid down by a prior convention that only certain moves and changes will count as parts of the game, and that all other distinguishable moves and changes are irrelevant to the game, and irrelevant to the account of the game. That certain changes are a change in the state of the game, in addition to being changes in the state of the world, is fixed by that system of conventions that constitutes the rules and purpose, and therefore the nature, of the game. For this reason some of the actual, perceptible movements of the pieces in chess, or of the ball and the players in cricket, have a significance within the game, while others have no such significance. A narrative of the game, considered simply as a game of chess and from no other point of view, will be correct and complete if it mentions only those moves in the game that are marked off by the rules as separate moves, each having a symbolic significance in the game. In the narrative of the game the first move or event of the game was so-and-so, the second so-and-so, each successive move being distinguishable by the rules as separate, and as properly occurring in one, and only one, place in the narrative. If one supposes that the narrative is not designed, as a narrative of the game, but as a narrative of what happened during the game, that is, a sequence of events that are not each marked off as separate moves; then no narrative can be complete and exhaustive in the sense that one could truly say at the end of it: 'And this is all that happened during that time', unless it had been previously indicated that only one class of event was to be recorded. Nor could one say, without qualification, that in any correct narrative of what happened during this period of time the same events would be mentioned. There is no rule of identity that would single out the different events as either the same or different independently of the possible alternative descriptions of them. Any one of an interminable set of true stories could begin: 'The first thing that happened was so-and-so, the next that happened was so-and-so', and yet each story would be different. Whatever was picked out as the first event in any particular narrative could be further sub-divided into a set of other events, and the dividing line between the first two events to be recorded, or between any subsequent two, could be differently placed. The account of the game can be determinate and complete, in its specially devised notation, only because the conditions of reference of its symbols have already been specified in ordinary language by the rules of chess. The preliminary abstraction has been made by the rules that specify what movement under what conditions is to count as a run in cricket, or as the movement of a pawn in chess. Since the physical movements themselves have a certain significance as signs, signifying a certain advancement in the game, the special notation that records the game is a symbolism at two removes from undistinguished reality, from mere Nature, unconventionalised and free from any social institution imposed upon it.

A musical score may also be compared with a language: suppose a simple statement of a melody. The written notes within the musical notation represent the tune with entire determinateness, if we neglect any indications of the manner of performance. The tune itself, apart from the representation of it, can be regarded as an abstraction from the sequence of sounds that would occur in any correct performance of it. The sequences of sound might be different from each other in other respects, although they were all performances of that particular tune. The written music may be taken as a representation of the tune as a tune, and any feature of the sequence of sounds that would count as a feature of the tune could be represented in the written music. All other features of the sequence of sounds could be neglected as not features of the tune. These are some of the conditions in which determinateness in representation can be achieved. But in language we must have devices for singling out the range of features of reality to which we refer at any particular time, since language, as the medium in which statements are made, is necessarily an indefinitely extendable system of signs, unlike a musical notation. The special, and artificially limited, notations themselves rest on this common basis of language, which provides the means of singling out a particular domain of interests. We have to supply the reference, and to state in words, how this representation is to be applied to some particular segment of experience, before we have an assertion before us that could be qualified as either true or false. When the

PERSONS AND THEIR SITUATION

reference to a segment of experience is supplied, it becomes
plain that any representation or description of it in any
form is always incomplete, in the sense that there is always
more that could be represented or described, and that is
left out of this particular representation.

If it is true that no limit can be placed on the variety of
objects of reference that may be singled out in reality,
then it follows that we cannot properly speak of the class
of all things that exist or of the class of all their properties.
There can be no rule for forming these classes. We can
properly speak, as in logic, of the class of all true statements,
since there is the possibility of prescribing criteria that any
utterance must satisfy in order to be called a statement.
There are no criteria that anything must satisfy in order
to be called a thing in the wide sense of the word. When
we survey the external world, we are looking at as many
things as we wish, and have the means, to distinguish. In
reporting what we find in the world, the only limit is to
be found in the resources of our vocabulary; and the only
limit to the extension of the vocabulary is the present
limit of our interests as co-operating and communicating
beings. The fundamental form of statement 'This is a so-
and-so' is the form of statement made when we are using
our eyes, our ears, our sense of touch, in conjunction with
the vocabulary of an established language, to identify
objects around us.

This same form of statement is also used in identifying
states of mind, attitudes, emotions, passions, moods. In all
these cases we necessarily distinguish the appearance from
the reality, how the thing or state manifests itself at the
particular time of speaking, the temporary impression that
it makes, from what it really is. There has always been a
natural tendency for philosophers to argue, first, that we

actually experience only these transitory impressions, and, secondly, that all our identifications of persisting things and states must be in principle paraphrasable as statements about the order of impressions or appearances. The tendency is natural, since it goes with the assumption that there must be natural, pre-social units already discriminated as the ultimate subjects of reference in our experience: that social convention and artificiality enters only at the second tier of language, resting on a first tier of basic and natural discrimination which is independent of any institutions of social life. Both the premiss and the conclusion of the argument are false. The premiss is false, since it is not true that the description that one might give of the impression or sensation of the moment is in any sense a more truthful record of 'experience' than is the identification of the object, unless one has previously defined 'experience' as that which is recorded in descriptions of this particular kind. If 'experience' were so defined, there would be no ground for saying that descriptions of 'experience', in this sense of the word, must be taken to be descriptions of what truly exists. On the contrary, experience would be most truthfully recorded in statements which only convey information about what seems to exist and which otherwise carry no existential commitment. When I feel angry, or when I see a horse, I may describe how the anger affected me on that particular occasion, and the sensations that accompanied it; and I may describe (in a great variety of ways) how the horse looked at that moment, from that angle, in that light, and to me, as opposed to other possible observers. It is typical of this kind of description, first, that many different descriptions might be given of the same experience, each of them conveying different aspects of the impression or sensation of the moment: secondly, that the speaker's doubt is rather as to which words will best convey the impression. He is typically challenged with the question 'Are you sure that that is the right word or phrase?' rather than with the question 'How do you know?': thirdly, that the expressions used will always be an adaptation of the vocabulary of identification, the adaptation being made by 'looks like so-and-so', 'felt as if so-and-so was happening' and so on. I may wish to describe the symptoms of anger, or the impression that the physical object made, for a variety of different purposes, and one of these purposes might be as an aid to the identification of the state of mind or the identification of the object. That I had exactly those same sensations which I ordinarily have when I am angry is often strong, but never by itself conclusive, evidence that my present state of mind is anger. That something looks to me exactly like a horse is often strong, but never by itself conclusive, evidence that it is a horse.

The principle of similarity here assumed in the phrases 'felt exactly like' and 'looked exactly like', or the principle of identity in 'same sensation' and 'same appearance', is never independently obvious and self-justifying. Similarity is always similarity in some or many respects. To say that I felt alike, or that I experienced exactly the same sensation, on two different occasions seems to imply that there is nothing that can be truly said in description of my sensation on one occasion that cannot be truly said of my sensation on the other occasion. Plainly some restriction on the type of description is presupposed here; and this restriction is implied in the word 'sensation'. 'Same sensation', 'same feeling', 'same look' each imply that, within a particular range of possible descriptions, the same descriptions can be truly applied to the two occasions. The range of descriptions intended is suggested by the words 'sensation', 'feeling', 'look': for only certain types of description count as descriptions of sensations. 'Same thing', 'same situation', 'same emotion' imply that, within a different and contrasted range of possible descriptions, the same descriptions apply on two occasions. In the same situation, or when subject to the same emotion, I may on two different occasions have different sensations; and I may experience the same sensations when my condition is very different, for example, when I am hungry and when I am frightened. We mark by 'same sensation' or 'same situation' the type of identity in description that is applicable. A sensation is not a type of thing, a thing that can be identified, as a situation is not a type of thing, a thing that can be identified. It makes no clear sense to say 'This is a sensation', and even less 'This is a situation', unless the type of sensation or situation intended is somehow indicated. Consequently 'same', as it occurs in 'same sensation' or 'same situation', does not have the same definite use as in 'same horse' or 'same man'. The question whether two men ever have the same sensation, or whether we ever find ourselves in the same situation twice, is not a determinate question, with a definite sense. This would only be a real question if there was a sense of numerically the same sensation, or numerically the same situation, corresponding to the sense of numerically the same horse. There is no principle of individuation attached to such concepts as 'situation' or 'sensation'. We cannot intelligibly ask how many situations, or how many sensations, there were. If we speak of the same situation, or the same sensation, lasting through some period of time, 'same' could always here be replaced by 'exactly similar'. We have no principle of individuation attached to these concepts by which we could distinguish 'one and the same one' from 'an exactly similar one in all relevant respects'. Even if I say that I have the same pain, as opposed to the same sensation, again, I do not regard this recurrence as part of the history of a persisting object—the pain. Similarly when I describe the appearance of a horse, as it presented itself to me at a particular moment, the visual impression that I received, I cannot speak of this impression or appearance as if it were a kind of thing with a history. On any occasion when I am conscious and alert and using my senses, there is no possibility of exhausting the variety of things that I may truly be said to be perceiving, and there is no possibility of exhausting the variety of true descriptions that might be given of my sensations. It cannot even be assumed that there are just two kinds of description of reality and experience, always neatly divided from each other, one being the description of subjective impressions and the other being the identification of objects in the external world. Descriptions of the look of things, of sounds, colours, tastes, smells, sensations and subjective impressions, may take many forms for many different purposes, some of them involving simultaneously an identification of the thing and a description of its momentary appearance. There is no very simple division. The verbs 'seems', 'feels', 'looks' and many others, together with such idioms as 'looks as if', provide a great range of intermediate descriptions, variously distinguished from each other in their uses and purposes.

There remains always the fundamental necessity that we should single out constant objects of reference in order to give sense to every other type of description. It would be impossible to make statements, either true or false, in a language that only tried to record the impressions of the moment. If one was confined to utterances of the form

'Here now red' or 'Here now pain', there would be no
method of determining that one so-called statement was
incompatible with another, and therefore no method of
establishing that any statement was either true or false.
'Here now red and green' would be an empty statement
unless there was a means of distinguishing the assertion that
the same thing is both red and green, and red and green in
the same parts of its surface, from the assertion that both
red and green are now visible. Even the statement 'Both
red and green are now visible' can only be interpreted if
'from some particular standpoint or standpoints' is presupposed. Tenses, as indications of the temporal relation
between an utterance and the topic of the utterance, could
not be interpreted without the possibility of a reference
to a persisting thing, which might be either the speaking
subject, or the subject of the statement. It is unavoidable
that any speaker or thinker should carry with him the idea
of referring to at least one persisting object, namely,
himself. With this idea he carries the idea of himself as an
object changing his standpoint and changing his relation
to constant objects around him, and to objects around him
changing in relation to himself. He can therefore attach
even his most impressionistic and subjective descriptions
to a particular position in space and time, and because of
this there arises the possibility of incompatible statements
referring to the same subject. Statements identifying
things, and their qualities and relations, could not possibly
be replaced by any set of descriptions of momentary
impressions. Rather the two kinds of statement—'It is
a so-and-so' and 'It looks to me now like so-and-so', and
the many variations of them—are complementary and
mutually dependent.

The two most general types of rule attaching words and

thoughts to reality are, first, the rule that singles out a so-and-so as the same so-and-so, the rule of identity: secondly, the rule that prescribes that anything resembling a particular thing, already singled out, in certain respects is also to be classified as a so-and-so, the rule of resemblance. All so-and-so's must resemble each other in some respect, the resemblance in that particular respect being the ground of the classification. It is also necessarily true that everything resembles everything in some respect. Of any two things whatever, there is some respect in which they can be said to resemble each other and not to resemble some third thing. We pick out resemblances in certain respects as the basis of our classifications and neglect other resemblances which, in pursuance of some new need or interest, may be marked later. We could go on picking out resemblances for ever, inexhaustibly; and to some extent we do, as we perpetually extend the vocabulary of a living language, or as we learn to move from one language to another, each recording different resemblances in vocabularies that do not always translate each other. Reality by itself sets no limit. The limit is set by changing practical needs and by the development of new powers and new forms of social life. The inertia of habit in using the vocabulary and grammar of actual languages also sets a limit. The familiar, inherited forms of language turn our attention towards certain kinds of resemblance and we cannot easily see through them and past them. We cannot return to a state of nature and to an innocent eye and, by a new social contract, start to build the institution of language again upon some rational principles. The existence of a language is already implied in the rational intention to form a new one. All innovations have to be made within the institutions already existing, and as a development of them.

It may seem that there is a primitive and natural sense of
resemblance that may be called 'resemblance in appearance', and that this natural resemblance is to be distinguished from resemblance in the more general sense of the
word. Things look alike or they do not look alike, they
sound alike or they do not sound alike, they taste alike or
they do not taste alike. It seems that we must perceive
such resemblances directly, that they *must* be noticed by
any observer, independently of the institution of a
vocabulary recording the respect of resemblance. Particularly it seems that the resemblance between two faces, or
between a photograph and the face that it represents, or
between a good naturalistic portrait and the sitter, is a
relation that always stands out as evident, independently
of any principle of classification or of any convention of
representation. And perhaps this is true; but it is difficult
to know what exactly one is admitting when one admits
this truth. It may be a fact that anyone presented with any
of these pairs of things would put them together in some
way as pairs, whether or not he had been introduced to
such resemblances before, or had had the basis of resemblance previously explained to him. Suppose that it is in fact
true that anyone, or almost anyone, would put them together in some way, seeing the resemblance immediately
and without the need to refer to any established principle
of classification: then the interest lies in the phrase 'in some
way'. As soon as anyone is given a complicated set of
things that are presumed to resemble each other in appearance, he has to adopt some principle or rule of arranging
them. The arrangement, or putting together, would otherwise be no more than arbitrary play without a means of
distinguishing success from failure in the arrangement. If
he is to *say* 'This is more like this than it is like this in

appearance', he will immediately realise that 'resemblance in appearance' has to be further specified, because there are an unlimited variety of ways in which things may resemble each other in appearance. The order 'Put all the things that resemble each other in appearance together in groups' would not be an intelligible order, and there would be no criterion of compliance with it, unless the kind of resemblance in appearance was suggested, either in words or by the circumstances in which the order was given. It may seem probable that exact or partial resemblance in colour would in fact everywhere and unavoidably be noticed and would be recorded in the vocabulary of every language. But that we should classify by shades of colour, as we do, rather than by intensity or saturation or texture, or by other properties of light-reflecting surfaces, is by no means unavoidable. A preliminary abstraction has been made, and it is not made in this form universally and necessarily and in every language. There will always be at any one time, and in any one culture, one, or several, standard types of resemblance in appearance, which have come to seem obvious and therefore 'natural'. Almost one might say that 'resemblance in appearance' comes to have a different meaning at different times, or, rather, that it is so vague and indeterminate in its conditions of application that it will be interpreted at one time in a manner which would not be understood at another time. In any society the concepts and forms of a language, together with forms of popular art, combine to fix in a stereotype the resemblances in appearance which we suppose at any one time that everyone at any time must always naturally notice. This is not to deny that there may be *some* resemblances in appearance that are in fact noticed and recorded in all known languages. Indeed I do not at this point intend either to assert or to deny any matter of fact: only to question the intuitive distinction between that which is natural and unlearnt and that which is social and learnt in the discrimination of resemblances. The notion of natural resemblance—looking alike, sounding alike, tasting alike, etc.—must be indistinct and blurred, because the opposition of natural and conventional here has no clear sense: for how can we say what resemblances we would still notice and wish to record, if we did not have any of those conventions of language, of drawing and of many other modes of representation, that we do in fact have? Here again is the self-refuting assumption of man in a partial state of nature, retaining one social institution, one means of communication and one set of conventions, but one that he has freely invented for himself, without the prior institutions, the means of communication and conventions, which would enable him to attach a sense to his invention. It is too late to make this effort of abstraction; and, even if it could be made, we would still wish to say that the types of resemblance in appearance that are not on this primitive list are just as much founded in the nature of things, waiting to be noticed, as are the primitive and universally noticed types of resemblance. Every imaginative extension of a vocabulary, bringing to attention types of perceptible similarity not previously marked, will always be called a discovery of a relation, or type of relation, which was always there waiting to be discovered. We find more in the nature of things, and in their appearance, the more variously we view them and classify them. The recording of discovered resemblances in our vocabulary allows us as much latitude in discriminating different facets of reality as does the identification of objects. The sensuous resemblances that we have occasion to notice, as we see and hear and touch

34

things, and the resemblances that we choose to notice between our sensations and states of consciousness at different times, form part of the grounds of our classification of things and states of mind.

In any discussion of classification, one returns always to colours, marked by the specific colour adjectives which, unlike almost any other adjectives, seem like names of the shades they stand for. The same, indiscriminable shade, precisely identifiable by its name, may recur again and again in experience. In the case of this isolable feature of experience, it seems artificial to speak of classification by resemblance, even exact resemblance. Specific colour adjectives, and indeed the whole system of colour description, are unique within the vocabulary in the conditions of their application. There are no other sensory predicates that are entirely determinate in the same sense: determinate, in the sense that there are a definite number of discriminable shades, to each one of which a definite name can be allotted. Philosophers have always been fascinated by the example of colour adjectives, and they have sometimes supposed that all descriptions of the phenomena of the senses or of introspection are, or could be, applied with almost equal determinateness. Specific shades of colour may be thought of as universals, in the traditional philosophers' sense, because exactly the same shade may be indicated as appearing at different times and in different places, as if we were referring to the same thing appearing at different times and places. But there are more differences, in addition to those already mentioned, in the way in which we refer to, and identify, shades of colour, and the way in which we refer to, and identify, a thing. We may say 'This (shade of) blue is the same shade of blue as that', but we cannot say 'This chair is the same chair as that', unless we mean that this chair is the same kind, or type, of chair as that. The double reference of the 'this' and the 'that' makes the statement of identity impossible, if the references are interpreted as references to particular concrete things. It is true that I can ask myself the question 'How many colours can I see and distinguish now?', apparently in parallel with the question 'How many chairs can I see and distinguish now?' But could there be a generally applicable method of determining either that I had, or had not, counted the same colour twice over? The chair, which I have counted twice, has a history, and I can show that I did in fact count it twice by filling in its history alongside my own history, between the two occasions. I cannot show that I have counted the same colour—as opposed to the same patch of colour—by filling in the history of the colour in question. It makes no sense to ask about a shade of colour 'What happened to this colour in the meantime? Did it move or change in any way?' One might try to write the history of a particular colour, explaining how it first came into existence as the result of an experiment, and how it was then used for this or that purpose at different times. But there would still be no sense in which the colour had, or could have, moved, changed or developed, and therefore there could be no history of its development. It is not even clear in what sense one could say that the colour, as opposed to a particular coloured thing, had come into existence at a particular date. It is characteristic of everything that can be said to have a history that it came into existence at a particular time, and that a method can be prescribed by which one might in principle discover when this particular specimen of its kind first came into existence.

It seems therefore that there must be one fundamental use of 'one and the same' which requires a persisting thing of some particular kind as a constant object of reference, a thing that has had a continuous history since it came into existence and that may have changed in the course of its history. For this use of 'same', we require some criterion of identity which must vary with every kind of thing singled out. Certainly the distinction between the use of 'same' that requires a criterion of identity through change, and the use of 'same' in 'same colour', cannot be made altogether sharp and precise, if we are trying to classify every idiom of ordinary speech accurately. We may single out in nature, or among artefacts, the same type, the same pattern, the same model, and inquire into the history of this particular type, pattern or model, as into the history of a particular specimen of the type. This is the sense in which we may speak of the same word and of its history in a language. A particular process or action, occurring at a particular time, may sometimes be regarded as a token specimen of a particular type of process or action, a type which has a continuous history of change and development since it first came into existence. Because the same type, pattern or model may have a more or less continuous history, without having the spatio-temporal continuity of a physical thing, we may be inclined to think of the type as no more than a set of characteristics attaching to the particular tokens or specimens of the type. There is no strict general rule to be found in the forms of language which will unfailingly mark these categorial distinctions, and no such definite rule is to be expected. One should rather expect a scale, or a variety of scales, with plain cases of expressions to be categorised in one way rather than another standing at either end of the scales. For the purposes of the present argument, the principle of ordering alone needs to be understood. Ordinary physical objects, and, more important, persons, are the plain and unavoidable cases of particular things that retain their identity through change. They are unavoidable, because a primitive vocabulary, apt for communicating men's immediate physical needs and social purposes, is largely a vocabulary of physical things classified by their socially recognised uses. Starting from this primitive basis, more and more sophisticated vocabularies single out more and more objects, some abstract, some concrete, as having a traceable history, even though these objects do not have that type of spatio-temporal continuity which is characteristic of physical things.

As there is no limit set to the kinds of resemblance that we may find occasion to notice in nature, so there is no limit set to the ways in which we may single out objects, or configurations of objects, as individuals persisting one and the same, with changing qualities, through a certain period of time. It is true that, having the forms of co-operation, and therefore the needs of communication, that we have, certain concrete and palpable things, both natural and man-made, stand out in the environment as units to be used and manipulated, marked out as units by their potential uses. A human being of the same structure and size, and having the same biological needs, would naturally make most of the same fundamental discriminations of enduring objects when he tries to attach his statements to reality by definite references. In any conceivable society he would be driven to refer to the same medium-sized objects, items in the furniture of nature ready for his use. But no definite line can be drawn between fundamental and natural objects, in this sense, and the types of identification that are not natural, except on the assumption that certain forms of social life and of co-operation are universal and necessary to men, and that they are in this sense natural. It may not be true, as a matter of anthropological fact, that the constant objects of reference in primitive communication are always concrete things. For philosophical understanding of the forms of thought, there is in any case no need to look for primitive man, even supposing that anthropology, as an empirical science, allowed that there was in fact a single recognisable type of primitive grammar and vocabulary.. The philosophical interest is only that the necessary features of any system of communication in which true statements can be distinguished from false should be distinguished from features of language that are contingent upon a particular social order. My argument has been that no feature of language can meaningfully be said to be natural, and unavoidable, unless it is shown to be a necessary feature of any system of communication in which true statements are distinguished from false; and then the proper word is 'necessary' and not 'natural'. Any language is part of a whole complex of social behaviour, and it is pointless to ask of this complex of behaviour as a whole, or even of any part abstracted from it, whether it is natural or artificial. It is 'natural', in the sense of necessary, to man to be a social being, and 'social' implies convention-observing, and 'conventional' is ordinarily opposed to 'natural'. We cannot now separate the world as we now see it, as a result of the infinitely complicated evolution of our ways of thought and speech as civilised beings, from the world as it really is, somehow divided into its elements by a 'natural' system of classification. We acquire in infancy the principles of individuation that now seem natural to us, together with early habits of manipulation and conventions of recognition, expression and co-operation. Starting from this assured base, we gradually come to single out other types of persisting things in our experience; and our experience is always itself being modified by the conceptual framework at all times imposed on it. At any time after infancy we are looking at a world already divided for us into persisting things of many different types, and with our attention already fixed upon a particular range of resemblances. In any man's experience, Nature has always been overlaid by, and approached through, a set of social conventions, the conventions of a language in being. He is born into a particular social order, which is as limiting as his position in the natural order. Scientific thought introduces new, consciously contrived and rationally defended principles of individuation, and original art endlessly brings to notice new resemblances which are outside the range of ordinary practical interests. The world is always open to conceptual re-arrangement. But the re-arrangement is only the addition of new tiers of discrimination to a foundation that remains constant: the recognition of persisting things singled out by active observers who have a statable standpoint as objects among other objects. It is in judgments of perception that the notion of identity, and principles of individuation, are given their earliest sense.

That beings, who are capable of action and observation, are born into, and move among, a world of persisting objects is a logical necessity and not a contingent matter of fact. Anyone who, following Hume, tries to describe the actual experience of beings capable of action, or even their experience in some imaginary world, as merely a succession of sensations at some point contradicts his own hypothesis. Whatever changes one tries to imagine in the nature of our perceptions, it would still be possible to single out persisting objects as objects of reference, and it would still be necessary, both for action and for communication. Below the level of communication in language and the making of statements, there is the act of intentional pointing, away from oneself and towards an object. The act of pointing is performed from a point of view and standpoint, which is the present situation of myself, as a persisting object placed among other objects. If we try to conceive a world in which this active gesture, with these recognised connotations, was impossible, we find that we are trying to imagine a type of experience that is not experience of an external world, that is, we are trying to imagine a world in which nothing is perceived. Perceiving is necessarily perceiving something external to the perceiver, and 'external' would have no sense if the perceiver did not have a situation and a point of view, which happens at a particular time to be his situation and his point of view. No sense can be given to the notion of a situation and a point of view, if the perceiver is not thought of as a self-moving object among other objects. It becomes impossible to understand how any identifiable object could be indicated, and therefore how any statement with external reference could be made, if the perceiver is thought of as an extensionless point, an unsituated consciousness, unable to make the distinction between 'here' and 'there'. As soon as the possibility of external reference is conceded, and therefore the possibility of marking the situation of the thing indicated in relation to the situation of the observer, the perceiver must be thought of as a persisting body among others.

Any act of communicating the presence of objects, any categorical statement that one may make about one's own perception of the environment, involves as part of itself some variant of the act of intentional pointing proceeding away from the perceiver to the perceived. When we say what we are perceiving, and when in this sense we make an identification, the statement can be contradicted in two ways: either it may be said that there does not in fact exist anything corresponding to the description that we give: or it may be said that, although there does exist something corresponding to our description, nothing of the kind is within the range of our perception now. Whatever description we give of something perceived, the thing must be in principle identifiable from more than one point of view. It must make sense to compare the look of it (or sound or feel) from one place or at one time with the look of it (or sound or feel) from another place or at another time. If the object of perception is not in principle identifiable from more than one point of view, it is possible only to produce the appropriate description of the sight (or sound or touch). The impression appears and disappears, and in the period of its duration may be compared with similar impressions, and by this comparison it earns one description or another. There is then no contrast between the momentary appearance of the thing, as perceived at one moment and from one point of view, and its real, or enduring, properties. Without this contrast any error made in the description of something perceived must be like an error made in the description of an organic, or inner, sensation. There could be no sense in confirming that the description, or identification, was correct by further observations and actions. We could not in any sense manipulate the object perceived and test its reactions or view it at another time or from another point of view. The word 'object' becomes out of place; the perception coincides with that which is perceived, as a bodily feeling coincides with that which is felt. This logical necessity would show itself in the impossibility of explicitly identifying that which is perceived in a statement of the form: 'This is a so-and-so.' One cannot properly say 'This is a pain', because no sense can be given to the reference of the word 'this'; what am I intentionally pointing to, and saying of it, independently identified, that *it* is a pain? One can only say 'I am in pain', as a fact about me at this moment. There is no corresponding fact about *the* pain, that it has appeared within my range of perception now. The pain itself has no identity to be established by tracing the history of its appearances. Therefore 'I feel a pain' comes to the same as 'I am in some pain'. Feeling is not here a species of perception. It is impossible to give a sense to perception, if there is no possible contrast between the aspect of the object that now presents itself and the object itself with all its properties, including those which are not now perceptible. Without this contrast, the ampliative form of statement 'This is a so-and-so' could not intelligibly occur. The whole force of a statement of this form lies in the step from the aspect of the thing referred to to the identification of it as a thing of a certain kind. It is a necessary truth that anything that can be said to be perceived should have some properties, which cannot be perceived at the same time as some others. This is a corollary of the necessary truth that any external object can in principle be perceived from more than one point of view. One cannot be said to identify the object perceived unless one is making a step from certain marks of recognition, however presented, to the nature of the continuing thing. If one is simply reporting the quality of the impression or feeling of the moment (e.g. 'I am feeling cold', 'I am feeling giddy'), the description will necessarily be incomplete as a description of how I am feeling at that moment. But there is no sense in which it is incomplete as a description of *that* impression or feeling. *That* impression or feeling has no independent existence or identity apart from this occasion.

43

It is only constituted as a separate subject of reference by the separate description offered on this particular occasion. Alongside the solid furniture of the world, concrete persisting objects, I may certainly perceive objects—flashes of lightning, rainbows, effects of light, and many others— to which the contrast of real and momentarily apparent properties does not apply; they can be referred to and identified through their spatial relations to concrete things and therefore to the observer.

Those philosophers who have written of perceiving 'sense-data' or 'sense-impressions' have found themselves compelled, against their will, to write as if a sense-datum or a sense-impression was a kind of thing, but a peculiarly evanescent kind. The concept of perception, which is as deeply rooted in language as the concept of knowledge itself, imposes this interpretation, when a noun or substantival phrase follows the verb 'perceive'. They find themselves inevitably confronting such questions as 'What is the principle of individuation for sense-data?' 'How long do they last?' 'Can they seem to have qualities that they do not in fact have?' 'Can two people perceive the same sense-datum?' They may try to dismiss these questions as misunderstandings, and to insist that by 'sense-datum' they mean only the appearances that things present to the perceiver, and they may insist that they are not another kind of thing. They may try to reject the implication that they must give a sense to 'same sense-datum' before the noun 'sense-datum' can be understood. They may claim that 'sense-datum' is only a noun of this kind by grammatical accident, a pseudo-noun. It is to be assumed that, in talking about sense-data, we will be talking, not about objects perceived, but only about their appearance, as perceived by some perceiver at some particular moment; an appearance is then not a kind of thing. But some of the conventions of grammar have deep roots and cannot be arbitrarily varied without correspondingly radical changes throughout the whole structure of a language. The contrast between the thing itself, and its appearance on any particular occasion as it presents itself to an observer, has to be expressed in a grammatical form that marks just this difference. We must have the contrast between the identification of the object perceived and the description of some impression of the object, as it appears to the perceiver now. This contrast runs through our language as a distinction between 'is a so-and-so' and 'seems, or looks like, or sounds like', and so on.

All perception of which we can form any idea is the perception of a finite observer moving among the objects that he observes from changing points of view in a common world. His language is addressed to other observers who are also perceptible objects also changing their point of view as they move in the common world. Every observer is aware of himself as one item in the furniture of the world, and, when he identifies the objects around him, he also thereby fixes in his own mind his own situation in the world. He could not either learn or consistently apply a vocabulary, unless he regarded himself as one self-moving observer among others, one body among other bodies, changing his own situation and limited range of observation. Many philosophers, in the tradition of Hume, have tried to represent the primitive or natural experience of a person, prior to active interpretation, as a succession of data, impressions or sensations, passively received and then compared by a mind that is detached from embodiment in any one position. It is then a contingent matter of fact that I perceive with my eyes, or receive tactual sensations through my hands, or through the surface of my body, touching other things. It is a contingent matter of fact that my visual or auditory sensations change as I move, or that I can always switch my observation from one thing to another, while I control my own body. It is a contingent matter of fact that I acquire my habits of identification in a social context, and therefore in communication with others, whom I perceive speaking to me from other points of view. But these are not contingent matters of fact, which can be dismissed as accidental and inessential to consciousness of objects. If one tries to imagine a kind of perception that does not conform to these conditions, and in which the body of the observer, movable at will, is not the medium of perception, one finds that the distinction between the perceiver and the object of perception has altogether disappeared; in consequence no sense can be given to the notion of perception under the supposed conditions. The line that we draw between 'inner sensations' and features of the external world depends upon this distinction between the active subject, who is a body among bodies, and who from time to time changes his own point of view, and the common object observed from many points of view. Tastes and smells lie on the border-line between perception and sensation, because, like objects of perception, there is a sense in which the same smell may be approached from different points of view, as the position of the observer is changed. But there is no ordinary sense in which the same smell can seem to be stronger than it actually is. We do not in this case speak of the changing aspects of the same smell, as perceived from different points of view, and therefore we also think of smells, unlike sounds, as sensations rather than perceptions, as 'inner' rather than 'outer'. Tastes are even less objects of percep-

46

tion than smells, since no contrast is allowed between what the taste is and what it may seem to be from a certain point of view. This is the contrast from which our apprehension of the external world must begin, as we work outwards from our own body, as constituting the centre of the universe, which is viewed from our own standpoint within it. We do not normally use tastes and smells to identify objects and to determine our own situation among objects, and, more important, we do not in our self-willed movements guide ourselves by taste and smell.

The deepest mistake in empiricist theories of perception, descending from Berkeley and Hume, has been the representation of human beings as passive observers receiving impressions from 'outside' of the mind, where the 'outside' includes their own bodies. In fact I find myself from the beginning able to act upon objects around me. In this context to act is to move at will my own body, that persisting physical thing, and thereby to bring about perceived movements of other physical things. I not only perceive my body, I also control it; I not only perceive external objects, I also manipulate them. To doubt the existence of my own body would necessarily be to doubt my ability to move. My own body is in action felt to be continuous with other resisting bodies, some of which can be made to move at will as my body moves; and many of the movements of my own body are simultaneously perceived, felt and willed. I find myself living in a medium of physical action and reaction, and I do not always need to infer from my observations alone that I have made a movement of some particular kind. I find my power of movement limited by the resistances of objects around me. This felt resistance to my will defines for me, in conjunction with my perceptions, my own situation as an object among other objects. Both perceptions and bodily sensations contribute to this elementary discovery; even taken together, they do not constitute the whole of it. I know directly, that I tried, or set myself, to move, or that I did not try, but was rather moved by something else. No knowledge is more direct and underived than this knowledge of the fact of my own intention to move or to bring about a change. It is therefore wrong to represent experience of the external world as some synthesis of impressions of each of the five senses. A physical object is recognised as a potential obstruction, or as something to be manipulated, occupying some definite position in relation to me at the moment of perception. The use of any of my senses, or any combination of them, gives me the means of recognising the obstruction, the thing to be manipulated, as of a certain kind and as liable to resist my intended actions in a certain way. Touch, and not sight, is primitively the most authoritative of the senses, the natural criterion of physical reality, just because acting upon objects necessarily involves touching, the contact of my body with the resisting body that is not my own. A perceived surface is a perceived point of potential resistance and obstruction. I may recognise the possibility and nature of the bodily resistance by the colour of the surface that I see. I may naturally use the form of words 'That is a coffee-jug', and, when asked what I am referring to, add 'That blue thing over there'. The expanse of blue, the so-called visual datum, may be the mark of recognition of the object; but the nature of the object itself is determined by the range of its possible manipulations, its possible actions and reactions in the context of standard social interests and of customary intentions. Nor is this true only of objects that are artefacts. Natural objects also are often distinguished and sorted into kinds by their powers, in Locke's terminology, and by their reactions to typical manipulations. Even when this is not true, and when physical objects are classified by their evident sensuous properties, the final criterion of their reality and actual existence is usually their palpability, their felt solidity as bodies resisting and complying with one's customary intentions. Admittedly, in sophisticated and scientific uses of language, one may speak of physical things that do not offer any perceptible resistance to the human body. This is one of the many respects—others will be noticed later—in which scientific descriptions are essentially those that are the least anthropocentric: they make the minimum reference both to standard human interests and to the standpoint of the observer. But these sophisticated objects of science still owe their status as bodies, and as objects existing in the external world, to their powers of affecting other bodies. The external world is a system of things displacing each other, acting and reacting upon each other, and, both in perception and in the least of my movements, I am aware of myself as one among these things. Therefore, when I am identifying the commonplace, socially recognised objects around me, I am identifying potential agents and reagents, taking their appearance, at the moment of identification, as a clue to what they are.

To state what a particular object is cannot be the same as to describe its appearance from various points of view. A description of the appearance of an object from a certain point of view only constitutes evidence as to what it is, when taken in conjunction with a statement of the actual situation of the observer as an object among other objects. For this reason the followers of Berkeley, the sense-datum philosophers, have always failed to show that statements identifying physical objects are translatable into statements

D

describing the actual and possible appearances of things. They have always found that their hypothetical propositions about sense-data could never be equivalent to categorical statements about actual objects, unless the protases of the hypotheticals specify the objective standpoint of the observer. Their mistake has always been not to acknowledge that the standpoint of the observer is one physical fact among others, and that the observer is always a self-moving body among other bodies which he observes and intentionally manipulates. They have asked 'How can we be said to perceive the real thing, as it is in itself, if its appearance is constantly changing under different conditions? Surely we cannot distinguish the object perceived from the whole range of its actual and possible appearances?' This is certainly a reasonable question, if the changing standpoint of the observer is not to be represented as a change of his situation *in* the world of objects, but as a change in his relation *to* the world from outside. The mistake is to assume that my only contact with objects, and with the world of physical things, is through perception, in which objects are presented to my passive mind.

I could perhaps maintain that I am aware of myself as a body solely through the impressions of the senses. I might argue that, when I move and act, I always verify by the sense of touch and by kinaesthetic sensations that I have moved and acted. Even if I say this, I cannot go further and argue that it is only by the sense of touch and by the other senses that I know that I possess a body, which moves at will, and that I am not merely a detached thinking being. I do not know how I would identify myself as a disembodied being, and I do not know what this hypothesis means. In default of the evidence of the senses, I may sometimes doubt whether I have succeeded in performing a particular action on a particular occasion. But I cannot doubt that there are *some* actions which, under favourable conditions, I *could* perform, even if I am in fact prevented by a physical cause from performing any of them. If I try to suppose myself to be incapable of acting in any way, and yet not to be prevented from acting by some physical cause, I virtually lose the possibility of distinguishing myself from anything else and any sense of my own identity as a person. If I lose so much as this, I lose the possibility of referring to anything in particular, and therefore of making any statement of fact. I distinguish myself from other things, first, as being in a certain situation, as being here rather than there, and, secondly, as being capable of planning to move from here to there. The thought of the possibility of changing my situation in the world among other objects is always present to me. Even at the most rudimentary stage of consciousness, I always distinguish that which I myself do with intention in changing my situation from that which happens to me. When I am not myself the agent bringing about some change in my consciousness, I must suppose it to have been caused by something external to me. The hypothesis of the disembodied thinker supposes both of these conditions of distinguishing myself from other things as removed. If one tries to suppose, following Hume, a form of experience that consists simply of a succession of impressions and ideas, one will be compelled to ask whether the subject can direct and control at will some of his impressions and ideas. If he cannot, how will he appear as a subject, a mind, a person, at all? If he can, must he not somehow distinguish the act of direction and control, which could not itself be counted as one more impression, or kind of impression, among the others?

The contrast between the person as the observer, fixing

his situation by reference to other things perceived, and the person as agent, altering his relation to other things at will, is a contrast which presents itself only when we reflect. In our ordinary awareness of things, we do not clearly distinguish our own voluntary movements among things, and our actions upon them, from the passive perception of them. Philosophers have tended to speak of the five senses as separate channels through which data from the external world are received. But touching, handling and the manipulation of things are misrepresented if we follow the analogy of vision, with which 'perception' is naturally associated. In handling and manipulating, we are not so much perceiving as acting. We often identify things as things of a certain kind by the particular pattern of action and reaction in our physical dealings with them, which are complementary to our perception of them, in the ordinary sense of 'perception'. It is essential to action that we should be in principle capable of discovering by observation whether we have in fact achieved that which we intended to achieve. Action and perception are in this way necessarily complementary and cannot be assimilated to each other. The manipulation of resisting objects, and the many other ways in which we physically act upon them, cannot be analysed in terms of a set of kinaesthetic and tactual sensations, even if intention, as an ingredient of action, is ignored; for the sensations that one may have while moving or manipulating an object are not in any case either necessary or sufficient to the identification of the movement as a movement of a certain kind, or to the identification of the action. The sensations that may accompany my actions and movements among things are, as it were, accidental, and not essential to the recognition of the actions and movements themselves. Certainly I may extend my hand to touch the surface of an object with a view to identifying the object by the sensation that I receive. But not all, or even most, handling and manipulation of objects can be thought of as the pursuit of tactual sensations. The manipulation often has a sense and purpose which looks towards a further reaction from the object. The whole complex of my action and the object's reaction may follow the expected pattern, or there may be something missing or unexpected. If there is something missing or unexpected, I might attend to tactual sensations or feelings as one element in the complex. But they are significant as evidence of what happened only within the complex, that is, as sensations occurring while such-and-such bodies are in contact in such-and-such a manner. It is my body that is the instrument of my intentions, whether they are disappointed or fulfilled.

We are in the world, as bodies among bodies, not only as observers but as active experimenters. We could not ever be observers unless we were sometimes active experimenters, and we could not ever be experimenters unless we were sometimes observers. To observe is to learn what obstructions there are in the environment: and to experiment is to act with a view to perceiving what happens when we act in a certain way. It is a commonplace that scientific knowledge generally comes, not from passive observation of the course of nature, but from observation of the results of deliberate interference. In this respect scientific exploration of the world is continuous with a child's exploration. A child may be watched fixing its relation to other things, and determining their nature, by experiment, that is, by observing the results of its calculated interferences. If one says that the child is learning to co-ordinate the look of things with its tactual sensations, this is true but incomplete; incomplete, because the child's own movements and actions are the constant background to this co-ordination. The look of things and the tactual sensations, and the co-ordination between them, only give him information about external things when taken in conjunction with his direct sense of his own movements and actions. This direct sense of his own initiated movements and actions is inseparable from his intention in making the movements or performing the actions. Intention is perhaps too rational and solemn a word when one is speaking of a child's experiments in movement. Certainly in ordinary adult life our direct sense of our own movements arises from our active intentions. I know directly whether I moved my arm or whether my arm moved of its own accord. My knowledge is not derived from some perception or sensation. I may perceive my arm moving, and at the same time know, but not perceive, that I did not move, or, regarding my arm as an external object, that I did not move it. My situation or place is fixed for me as the place *from* which I move my arm or other limbs, which is also the place *from* which I see and move things around me. As I move at will, my point of view correspondingly changes, and it is in this way that I explore the world arranged around me as its centre.

My references to things in my environment are, in the last resort, explained to someone else by my pointing to, or handling, the thing referred to. This natural, pre-social gesture, performed with intention, is the link on which all communication about physical things ultimately depends. It seems that no social convention is required to make this gesture intelligible, even though a rudimentary intention is incorporated in it. Even the etymology of the word 'intention' suggests that the gesture of pointing from a place to a place is the natural and concrete expression of intention. Pointing, either with arms or head or any limbs or instruments, has a natural sense and direction, and therefore a natural, indeterminate meaning—'From me to this'. Something which under no conceivable conditions could be pointed to or handled would not be a physical thing. I must be able, at least in some ideal circumstances, to locate the thing referred to by a natural gesture, and say 'This, which I am pointing to now, is a so-and-so or the so-and-so'. Certainly pointing is a fallible procedure and the reference of my gesture may always be misunderstood. I may at any time be thought to be pointing to something, or to some feature of something, other than that which I in fact intended. Without a context in which social conventions, including some of the conventions of language, have narrowed the possibilities, the gesture always remains indeterminate. But, if communication is to be possible, it must be in principle possible to anchor my statements to commonly perceived and persisting things by this natural gesture, however difficult it may be to explain, in particular cases, which thing, or feature of a thing, I am in fact referring to. If I refer to something in the external world, which could not in any circumstances be pointed to, then it will be necessary for me to explain how this putative thing is related to something that might be pointed out to my interlocutor under prescribed conditions.

For all these reasons an absolute distinction must be drawn between the things and persons that constitute the external world and the sensations or impressions that I or anyone else may from moment to moment enjoy. It must be a mistake to try to show that, in referring to external things, we are indirectly referring to the order of our sensations. The truth is rather that I have to explain my references to my own sensations and impressions by references to the physical things or events with which they are in some way associated. In order to communicate to someone else, or to record for myself, the fact that I had a certain sensation in touching something, or that things presented some peculiar appearance to me at a particular moment, I inevitably bring in some reference to physical things, both in describing accurately the sensation or impression and also in fixing the occasion on which it occurred. Even in the most simple case, when I am describing for myself alone my sensations and impressions, as they occur, my description will necessarily involve a comparison with earlier sensations, and a comparison in certain respects only. I will therefore need to distinguish the occasions on which the past sensations occurred, and I could not make this distinction simply by referring to the past sensations themselves. If I have to compare two sensations, using a word that marks their similarity in a certain respect, then I have to say that they each resemble each other in some respect in which they both resemble a third but in which they do not resemble a fourth. This is the only way in which I can fix the meaning of my descriptive word, either for myself or for anyone else. It may seem that I only need to recall the past sensations in my own mind. Certainly this may in many cases be enough to satisfy me that my present sensation does in fact properly fall under the same classification as some past sensation. But, in setting up my vocabulary for describing my sensations, I will necessarily introduce *rules* of the form 'the *same* sensation cannot be said to be both so-and-so and so-and-so at the same time'. In default of rules of this form, my association of a word with a present sensation will not count as a true or false description of that sensation. The mere recital of the word, when the sensation occurs, will not count as a statement *about* that sensation, a statement susceptible of being either true or false, unless there are rules, which I would formulate, if my meaning was questioned, and which determine the compatibility and incompatibility of the predicates involved. Rules determining the compatibility of predicates are only applicable if there is some principle of individuation attached to the subject-terms with which the predicates are to be linked in statements. Therefore the possibility of describing my sensations, and of my making statements about them, is inseparable from my giving some sense to 'one and the same sensation'; and *ex hypothesi* 'one and the same' cannot here mean 'an exactly similar one'. In order to identify the sensation, I would be driven to speak of 'the sensation that was caused by so-and-so' or 'that occurred at the same time as so-and-so'. The principle that I would use in identifying the past sensation would be drawn from its connection with external things. I would not therefore be in a position to describe my sensations unless I also had in my language the means to identify and to describe external objects.

This argument is entirely general and does not allow exceptions. If anyone claimed that he had discovered a people speaking a language in which only sensations were referred to and described, he would be claiming something that could not possibly be true. It must at least be possible in this supposed language for the speakers to discriminate one person from another; if they have the means to do this, they already have the means to discriminate one object in the external world from another. Persons are, among other things, objects occupying space in the external world, and discriminated from each other, partly at least, in the way in which other physical objects are discriminated from each other. If we try to imagine that no discrimination between persons is in principle possible in the supposed language, and that a speaker can only announce some description of his own sensations, then we are imagining a language in which contradiction by another person of any statement made is in principle impossible. It would also be a language in which pronouns would have no sense. The so-called description of a sensation would be meaningless to anyone other than the speaker, and would involve no possible intersubjective comparison. A language without the possibility of communication would be a language at vanishing-point. Statements that can only be discarded, in the sense of not repeated, but can never be contradicted, would be statements at vanishing-point. There would be no criterion by which the social act of making a statement could be distinguished from an utterance constantly provoked by a recurring stimulus. Each speaker of this 'language' would be regarding himself as an island, and not as a person in the world, seeing it from his own point of view and describing it within the conventions of his society. The idea of his own point of view, as one point of view among many others that might have been his, would in no way be reflected in his language. The structure of language, as we know it, is built upon the fact that each speaker speaks to an actual or potential hearer, marking the point of view in space and time from which he speaks. The very idea of communication between persons involves this necessity of the speaker marking his point of view by devices of attachment, such as pronouns, demonstratives and tenses, and also the possibility of his pointing from his own situation to things and persons in his environment. Even if he wishes to speak entirely about himself and about his own feelings and sensations, he will still be speaking about himself as one person among others, identifiable as having a particular position and history. His own feelings and sensations occurred in conjunction with other independently identifiable events and situations in his history, while he was in such-and-such a position or performing such-and-such actions. He has to exteriorise, as it were, his sensations in order to refer to them and to describe them at all. They have to be fitted into the framework of a narrative, the narrative of his life, which must cross the narrative and history of other things and persons at many points.

Nor is this need of exteriorising one's own sensations merely a necessity of language and of description, as idealist philosophers have argued. Whatever I feel, my feeling occurs in conjunction with my doing something, or perceiving something, or my being in some way conscious of my situation in the world. Admittedly there may be moments in my life, awaking from sleep or from an anaesthetic, when I am aware only of certain sensations and impressions and not aware of my own situation in the world. If I try at such a moment to describe what is happening to me, or what I am doing, I will necessarily fail, under the conditions supposed. If I do not know, even in the most vague outline, what my situation is in relation to any object whatever, it is logically impossible for me to describe what I am doing or what is happening to me. It may be thought that at least under these conditions I can describe my own impressions. But even this is a mistake, or at least needs qualification. Whatever my impressions were, I could not know that they were mere sensations of mine, unless I knew that what seemed to be happening to me in this semi-awakened state was not really happening to me. At the most I might perhaps make statements of the kind 'I feel cold', 'I am in pain', 'I feel giddy', statements which carry the least possible implication about my actual situation. These statements so far imply only a disposition or tendency to behave in a certain way. As soon as I went beyond relatively unspecific statements about organic sensations, I would need to know that what I was describing as my sensations really were sensations only. I would need at least to know that I was awake and lying in a room before I could be sure what I was feeling, or, rather, that any classification of my feelings was correct. In general, when I speak of my own feelings and sensations, I have to make some contrast between actual, perceived changes in my body or my environment and mere sensations. Perhaps my organic and bodily sensations can be mentioned in a narrative of my experiences, as part of my history and as isolated facts, with only the minimum implications about my situation in the world at the time. Organic sensations are not in any sense perceived; they simply occur. One has the sensations; one does not perceive them. Therefore there is no question of the point of view from which they are perceived. But in normal life they occur at the same time as, and are described in conjunction with, my concurrent perceptions and actions and with the impinging of external things. Our vocabulary, particularly the verbs, naturally enable us to record these composite occurrences, the sensation together with its typical cause or occasion. In the abnormal circumstances just supposed, when I am aware of absolutely nothing that I take to be an object in the external world, I may be compelled to attend to my sensations alone in abstraction from everything else. If I am aware of this as a compulsion, that is, if I know that I cannot perceive anything of the external world, however much I try, I already know something of my real situation in the world, and I am in a position to describe my sensations as sensations.

Ordinarily I single out my sensations, as objects for attention and description, from the mass of my contemporary perceptions, actions and reactions, when, as pleasant or painful, they demand attention and description. They demand attention, only as demanding action, either with a view to prolongation or avoidance. They are my sensations only in contrast to my perceptions of the external world, the world of objects to which I can point as being at some distance from me. When I describe my sensations more specifically, I must ultimately make clear to myself and to others the resemblances that I find by saying, either to myself or to others, 'I feel now exactly as I felt when so-and-so was happening: and exactly this feeling, which occurred on these identifiable occasions, is what I call feeling x (e.g. cold, giddy, etc.)'. In making the comparison I must hold in mind the respect in which I find a definite resemblance between my feelings on the two occasions, a resemblance that will lead me into further comparison with other occasions. We are only inclined to believe that the same sensation has a sense as something intrinsically identifiable, without reference to anything else, because we take the phrase 'I feel now exactly as I felt when doing so-and-so' as a complete statement. In a sense it is like a complete statement in the sense that it communicates something to the hearer: for it seems that there might have been no noteworthy and recognised resemblance between what I feel now and what I was feeling when I was doing so-and-so, at the most only a very far-fetched and unimportant resemblance. 'Far-fetched and unimportant' has a sense in the context of possible action, or of reasons for action, of prolongation of pleasure and avoidance of pain. But still nothing has so far been said about *what* the feeling is and was. Even if it is only further specified as 'a particular kind of pain', the statement will be in some circumstances open to challenge, or may demand further reflection, on the grounds that 'pain', as opposed, for example, to 'discomfort', does not altogether fit the case. If I say merely that I now feel in some ways rather like what I felt when I was doing so-and-so, I will not have said anything until I have picked out what the resemblance is. There are indefinite possibilities of finding analogies between my total state on one occasion and another. But of the possible analogies, only those enter into consciousness as noteworthy, and acquire social recognition in language, which are possible motives for movement and action.

Looking through the spectacles of our established vocabulary, and of the conventions of social life that are its background, certain resemblances and analogies of feeling seem more 'natural' and inevitably noticed than others. But there are only one or two resemblances that we can expect to find recorded in every vocabulary, provided that it allows personal disclosures of any kind. These are the resemblance between states that are painful, and the resemblance between states that are pleasant. When we disclose a pain, we necessarily suggest that our feeling is something to be avoided and that, other things being equal, we want, and have a reason, to escape from it. When we disclose that we have a pleasant feeling, we imply that, other things being equal, we want, and have a reason, to prolong the feeling. The word 'pain' is constantly used as an example by contemporary philosophers when they are discussing the interiority of inner life and the difficulty of describing it. Yet in fact the word 'pain', and also the word 'pleasure', constitute altogether special cases. Although 'pain' is in most of its uses a word that applies to sensations, and 'pleasure' in most of its uses applies rather to states of mind and feelings, they are alike in the implication, which is part of their meaning, that the subject to which they are applied has a reason for acting. It would be unintelligible to admit that someone derives pleasure from something and at the same time to deny that he has any reason for seeking it. It would be unintelligible to admit that something is painful and at the same time deny that there is any reason for avoiding it. 'Pain' is the only word applicable to sensations that has an entirely definite, though unspecific, sense, just because it directly indicates a reason for action. Pains are of many different kinds and it is very difficult to find any way of describing and classifying them. The difficulty that we find in conveying the particular quality of a painful sensation is not a trivial difficulty, but rather a difficulty of principle. It is easy to indicate a negative reaction to a sensation by describing it as a pain, just because so little specific information is thereby communicated, except this disposition of the person to avoid whatever it is that he is feeling. But in order to communicate or record the kind of pain that I am feeling, I will be driven to refer to the types of situation with which this feeling is generally associated in my experience: 'I feel as I feel when doing so-and-so, or when so-and-so is happening to me.' If in my vocabulary there are single words or phrases that describe particular kinds of pain, the meaning of these words or phrases will be explained as 'the kind of painful sensation that one has when so-and-so is happening'.

That sensations cannot easily be singled out as objects by themselves, without any attachment to a person's whole situation, is not merely a contingent feature of the structure of our language. The forms of language, and the way in which we learn and apply sensation-words, illustrate the fact that our perceptions are those of a person moving and acting within the world of objects that he perceives, and aware of his own identity as a thing alongside other things. In dreaming I may lose my sense of my own identity as a thing occupying a particular position in space at a particular time. In a dream all things are possible, because both the dreamer, and the objects and persons about which he dreams, may change their nature and their position without any continuity being preserved. Dreams for this reason have always been the model of unreality, with the essential conditions of perception reversed. Except in extreme cases of madness, the hallucinations and illusions of waking life occur against a stable background of real objects perceived and identified, and the perceiving subject never altogether loses his accurate sense of his own situation in relation to some at least of the objects around him. Dream is total hallucination, and the dreamer wakes up to find that there is no continuity between the place that he occupies now and the place that he seemed to occupy when, as he now realises, he was asleep. This total discontinuity in my sense of my own position is a necessary condition of my dismissing my experience as a dream. 'Waking up' is the name for the process of becoming aware of the discontinuity. This continuing awareness of my own position in the world is the foundation of self-consciousness.

Most human thought and feeling is necessarily directed outwards towards the environment in which we are situated and upon which we act. The vocabulary of emotions, attitudes, moods, states of mind and feelings requires that we identify our thoughts and feelings at least partly by reference to the public occasion and the circumstances of my situation at the time. But there is an important difference in the conditions of communication of thoughts and feelings. Thoughts can always be put into spoken or written words, and, in being put into words, are directly communicated. I give you my thoughts in stating them: nothing need be left uncommunicated. The thoughts can be completely identified by the expression of them. The thoughts are in the words and nothing need be left behind the words. I do not give you my feelings in describing them. Even images are images of things that are objects of common reference, and, however difficult it may be to describe the distinctive features of my imagery, I can at least record what my images are images of. But moods, states of mind, feelings and sensations have to be described, the particular quality of them communicated; and to find more and more effective ways of describing them is the most serious of all the necessary refinements of language. It is serious, because moods, states of mind and feelings must be distinguished and identified in a society before they can be facts that enter into men's practical intentions and manners. Every variety of analogy and metaphor is called into play, and, in this use of language we cannot be sure in advance that we will succeed in communicating, in making ourselves understood. There is no certain method and we cannot rely entirely on the publicly established rules of a vocabulary. The mark of success is that a description, which was originally a metaphor or a description by analogy, becomes standardised, and therefore almost literal, because it makes the comparison that is generally accepted in a society as a natural extension of the language. However successful one may be in suggesting to others how one feels by some analogy, there is still no sure way of identifying recurring states of consciousness except by some reference to the recurring situations in which they are enjoyed, and to the behaviour which is their natural expression. That I like or dislike something, that I want it or want to avoid it, are facts about me that are as definite as the fact that I am standing in a certain position. They are my half-observed and half-disclosed dispositions and have their recognised and conventional expressions in gesture, movement or words. The difficulty begins when one tries to regard one's own states of mind and feelings as identifiable objects of attention. One can never altogether succeed. I may self-consciously watch my own anger or disappointment growing, or attend with care to my own bodily sensations, noting and describing their changes. Yet when I try to describe the felt quality of my experiences, putting my intimate feelings into words, I must always have the sense that the words fall short, that any description can only be indefinite and untestable and liable to mislead. This is because feelings cannot be thought of as objects which can be surveyed by different observers from different points of view and which, when surveyed from one point of view, may seem to be other than they are. I cannot therefore pick them out as separate entities and label them and give an inventory of my feelings at any particular time. The kind of determinateness and precision that I can attain in describing myself or another person as an object among other objects, or as an agent acting upon other objects, cannot be attained when I try to separate my inner experiences from my environment. I am then no longer referring to socially recognised behaviour, and I am trying in my descriptions to go beyond any conventional classifications.

The argument of this chapter has been that it is a necessity in the use of language that we should refer to persisting objects, employing some criteria of identity through change: it is a necessity that the speaker should have the means of indicating his own point of view or standpoint, since he is himself one object among others; that every object must exhibit different appearances from different points of view: and that every object, including persons who are language-users, agents and observers, has a history of changing relations to other things in its environment. These truisms entail consequences in the theory of perception, the theory of mind, the theory of action. One must in philosophy consider human beings simultaneously as observers and as agents and as language-users. If one considers the theory of mind and ethics separately, both are apt to be falsified. The forms of our languages are largely determined by our practical interests as social beings: and our practical interests, the goals of action, are limited by our powers of communication and description. Within language as we know it, a limit is set to the possibility of varying the forms of language, and of varying the ways in which we think about our own actions, by our nature as perceiving and thinking beings who are also intentional agents moving among other things. One must start from the truisms that state these limits, whether they are expressed as truisms about language as an institution, or as truisms about the human mind in its relation to the external world. We cannot claim an absolute and unconditional finality for these truisms, since the deduction of them is always a deduction within language as we know it. But the deduction only shows that we are not in a position to describe any alternative forms of communication between intentional agents which do not exemplify these truisms.

It is important that in philosophy one should not represent human beings as observers standing outside the world. It lies in the nature of philosophical inquiry that this should be the temptation, since in philosophy one is trying to survey the human situation from some more independent standpoint, dividing that which is in some sense given in the nature of things and is necessary from that which is contingent upon changeable human convention. A philosopher is then liable to adopt a god-like pose, as if he had some independent insight into the necessary divisions in reality.

No description of things around me can be complete and final: no communication of feelings, or insight into the feelings of another, can be ideally complete and ideally adequate. Therefore no reckoning of the consequences of any of my actions can be ideally complete and final. It must be considered surprising that we can make these philosophical statements and claim to understand them and believe them to be true. We cannot have formed an idea of that which we assert to be beyond our reach, of what complete knowledge would be like or of what completely responsible action would be like. We arrive at these limiting ideas by extrapolation. We look for knowledge that is more and more objective, and less and less limited by our particular standpoint, and we look for action that is more and more responsible and less and less blind and uncontrolled. Rather than vacuously imagining perfection it is more constructive to recognise the necessary imperfection of our knowledge and of our powers of responsible action, and to mark the paths of improvement within these necessary limits.

Thinking and the making of statements are the activities of a person who is surrounded by identifiable objects to which he can refer. There is one continuing object about the existence and identifying features of which he is never in doubt and which he can always use as a fixed point of reference: himself. However uncertain he may be in referring to things in his environment, he can always identify himself as the man who is doing, or trying to do, so-and-so. He is aware of himself as the centre from which all his perceptions radiate, and he is aware that, as he moves or is moved, his perspective changes. Intentional movement gives him his sense of being in the world, and prevents him from thinking of himself as a neutral point, outside the world, to which things or impressions are presented in one single natural order. He could not think of his experience of the external world as a succession of impressions and ideas, unless he thought of his own movements as mere impressions also. Then he would have to think that the correlation between changes in one type of impression (his bodily sensations) and changes in the other (the data of external sense) was merely a contingent and surprising matter of fact. It is difficult to conceive how he would then distinguish some movements of his body as his own movements, his actions as his own actions. The most unavoidable feature of our consciousness is the initiation of change at will, the changing of position and therefore of our relation to other things. Even a man totally paralysed from birth would perhaps move his eyes and would form from his own experience some idea of the experience of moving at will. The idea of a thinking observer who could form from his experience no notion of making a movement, or, more generally, of doing something, is one that can scarcely be entertained, if one tries to follow its implications through to the end. For instance, he would have no reason to make any kind of identification of himself with his body, as 'his' body would only be for him one physical object among others. Yet his sense-organs are part of his body, and it must be presumed that he uses and directs them at will; or, if we suppose that he does not, 'observation' loses its sense. I am not here concerned with the facts that might be disclosed by a psychologist studying exceptional cases of paralysis, but only with the necessary interconnection of the concepts of action, observation and personality. Considering only the concepts of observation, action and a person, it may be true that there is no outright contradiction in the notion of a particular person who in fact remains throughout his life an almost totally inactive observer; it is rather that the idea breaks down and shows itself inconceivable, if we try to suppose a man who has acquired no conception of action at all and who thinks of himself as an observer of the external world. The totally paralysed man uses the language of active observers, and therefore understands the possibility of moving, and of thereby necessarily changing his point of view with every change of his position in the world. It is essential to the idea of an action that a person's knowledge that an action of his is his own action is not the conclusion of an inference. I may make the movement deliberately, having in view the result that I intend. The result may be exactly that which I envisaged and intended, or there may be a divergence between the intention and the actual outcome of my movement. This experimentation—in the original sense of 'trying'—is my most primitive and inevitable dealing with the world, and my most primitive and inevitable thinking, at least as primitive as the thought that expresses itself in the making of statements. Some of the most fundamental categories in our verbal thinking can be traced to these acts of calculated movement and manipulation and to the necessities of thought that accompany them. First, it is in movement, and particularly in voluntary movement, that temporal intervals, before and after, impose themselves as the necessary forms of all experience. The future is that which is in principle alterable by action, the past that which is in principle unalterable by action. Even when I know that something in the future is unalterable—for example, tomorrow's sunrise—I can intelligibly inquire into the steps that one would need to be able to take in order to prevent it; and this would be the same as to inquire into the causes of the event. If I ask what steps I would need to take to prevent somebody from being killed, who, unknown to me, has already been killed, an account of the causes of his death will tell me what I would have needed to be able to do in order to prevent it. But I would not appeal to this account in order to explain why his death is a fact that I must accept as unalterable. I would appeal to the evidences of his death, and not to its causes. The notions of causality and alterability, and of knowledge of fact and unalterability, are already established together with the notion of action.

When I make a movement or initiate a change myself, or when I perceive something moving or changing, I distinctly perceive the relation of before and after, the lapse, in the same sense that I directly perceive the things or qualities that are changing. It has been a fault in empiricist philosophies that the idea of the past, and of knowledge of the past, has been made to seem derivative and mysterious. This is partly because human experience has been represented wholly in its passive forms in terms of the 'data' of consciousness passing like a film before the impassive observer. It is made to seem primitively natural that we should have names of the qualities of impressions received, but somehow less primitively natural that there should be verbs as names of processes initiated and enjoyed. In making a movement, I do not normally think of myself as

71

remembering the early stages of the movement. The whole of the movement is embraced in the intention—'going, going, gone' as I move my hand, or as I move an object from my field of view. I could not even begin to conceive what it would be like not to have this immediate sense of before and after in movement and action, as the condition of all my experience as agent and observer. Because I always have intentions, and because knowing what I am doing at this moment necessarily involves knowing what I have just done and knowing what I am immediately about to do, my attention does not rest in the present. Memory, deliberate recall of the past, is generally invoked only when there is some form of discontinuity between that which I am doing and suffering now and that which I was doing or suffering before. I am not now doing what I was doing and therefore I may need to remember. But 'discontinuity', relevant to present intention and action, cannot here be given any very exact sense: it is a matter of degree, vaguely marked only. Sometimes I may admit that I have forgotten, not only what I was doing a few minutes ago, but even what I *am* doing at this moment. In such a case I know that my present actions, narrowly defined, are in intention continuous with the actions that preceded them in such a way as to constitute a single continuous action. I have forgotten what the single, unifying intention was, and have therefore forgotten the sense and direction of my present action. Ordinarily we carry our intentions with us, and this carrying forward of intentions, together with the perception of movement, provides the natural and necessary continuity of our experience. Any action, as an intended bringing about of an effect, has a certain trajectory, a relation of before and after within it. This continuity of an intentional action gives the assurance of my own existence as a continuing object of reference. 'I did it', as opposed to 'It just happened' or 'Someone else did it', is the primary, unquestionable indication of my own, utterly distinct existence as an object of reference. In this act of referring to myself as the source of an action, and of referring to myself intentionally, I have that peculiar guarantee of my own distinct existence that Descartes put into the Cogito. The guarantee lies in the intention behind the act of reference, an intention that I could not mistake for anything but my own.

One is in this way prevented from thinking of the present as a razor-edge, or as without the possibility of temporal division. The stretch of measurable time that may be referred to by the word 'now' is as indeterminate and elastic as is the range of 'present action' or 'present situation'. There could be no temptation in experience to think of the present as a point-instant. The 'continuous present' is the name naturally given to the tense that we use in describing our actions contemporaneously. A human being's action is normally constituted of means towards an end; it is a bringing about of some result with a view to some result. 'With a view to', or 'in order to', are unavoidable idioms in giving the sense of the notion of an action, the arrow of agency passing through the present and pointing forward in time. We are always looking at the present situation as arising from the immediate past by some agency, and as passing into some other situation by some force or agency that is operative now. The categories of causal explanation have in this way their roots within our own experience of ourselves as agents. One might perhaps try to imagine a kind of psycho-kinesis, in which I willed certain changes in the world, including changes in my own body, and in which some of these changes invariably happened as I willed. But if nothing outside the mental act of willing itself could ever show that I had willed a certain change, what would discriminate willing this change to occur from merely *thinking* of it as possible, or as desirable or likely? It will be no answer to say that I know myself by introspection whether I willed it or merely thought of it as desirable. If I do not *do* anything extra when I make the transition from thinking of it to willing it, I might just as well say that the mere thinking of the change as desirable brings about the change. Then either I could not fail to bring about any change that I wanted, or the original correlation between my will and its effects could never be established.

From the experience of action also arises that idea of the unity of mind and body, which has been distorted by philosophers when they think of persons only as passive observers and not as self-willed agents. An ordinary human action is a combination of intention and physical movement. But the combination of the two is not a simple additive one. The movement is guided by the intention, which may not be, and often is not, distinguishable as a separate event from the movement guided. I know that my action is performed at will, and I know what I am trying to do. But this does not necessarily imply that there has been some distinguishable mental event which was an act of will. I often cannot, in reflection or introspection, distinguish as separable episodes the thought of what is to be done from the actual doing of it. A philosophical dualism, which supposes that my history is analysable into two parallel sequences of mental and physical events, does not give a possible account of the concept of action.

Even when there are other thoughts running in my head parallel with my actions, the actions themselves are governed by an intention that enters into the action and that differentiates it from mere physical movement. We have therefore no reason to look for some criterion of personal identity that is distinct from the identity of our bodies as persisting physical objects. We find our intelligence and our will working, and expressing themselves in action, at a particular place at a particular time, and just these movements, or this voluntary stillness, are unmistakably mine, if they are my actions, animated by my intentions. I knew that I was in that situation, surrounded by some recognised objects, at that particular time, seeing things from that particular point of view and with those active intentions. Perhaps my thoughts and intentions were directed towards something remote from my environment, or perhaps I was daydreaming. I can only be said to have lost a sense of my own identity if I have lost all sense of where I am and what I am doing. Then I must have lost consciousness, since consciousness simply consists in knowing what I am doing. For any given moment or period in my existence, conscious or unconscious, there must be some set of possible true answers to the question, 'What were you doing, or where were you, then?' even if the answer mentions only my situation ('I was unconscious on the floor'), and not any conscious activity. A man's life is completely divided into periods during which he was conscious, and in respect of which there is therefore an answer to the question 'What was he doing?', and periods in which he was not conscious and therefore the only answerable question was 'What was his situation?' It is logically impossible that there should be any interruption in this smooth succession of situations and activities which constitutes my history. If it is admitted there was an interruption, a period of time in respect of which no true answer can be given to the question 'What were you doing then, or what happened to you?', it is admitted that the person originally referred to perished, and that another person, perhaps exactly like him in many respects, came into existence in his place. Every possible answer to the question 'What were you doing, or what happened to you, then?' carries some implication, even if only a negative one, about the person's situation at the time, as an object among other objects: a 'negative implication', in the sense that it is always possible to specify some statement about the external situation, which, if it were true, would be incompatible with the account given of what I was doing or undergoing, whatever this account might be. My account of my situation and activities at any particular time must fit into the account that independent observers would give both of my motions and overt expression at that time and of the state of my environment. If I begin by reporting merely my sensations and undirected moods—that I was in pain at the time and feeling anxious—I have committed myself to a minimum negative implication about my situation and circumstances at the time. It might emerge that I was asleep at the time, and that the pain and the feeling that ordinarily accompanies anxiety must have been part of a dream. In that case it would not be part of my history that I felt pain and was feeling anxious at that time. That I dreamt that I was in pain would be part of my history and that I experienced anxiety in my dream. Even my most intimate experiences occur against the background of my total situation at the time, and, when I classify the experiences as being of one kind or another, and as part of my history, I necessarily take into account the background and total situation. If I choose to describe my sensations, feelings or emotions subjectively, trying only to communicate the quality of the experience as it appeared to me at the time, I may perhaps avoid committing myself in any way, even by implication, about my total situation at the time; I may succeed in saying only what seemed to me at the time to be my situation, and what it felt like. Speaking, as it were, from the inside outwards, I may ignore both the outward expression of my feelings and the public occasion with which they are connected. But I do not by this effort of abstraction create for myself the illusion that the inner life of my feelings is cut off from their bodily expression, their causes, or the external occasion of them. I simply concentrate attention on one aspect or feature of my total situation. This is made clear to me particularly by the intentions, the actions and reactions, that arise out of my feelings; and 'arise out of' here represents something more intimate than a causal relation. If I am in pain, I generally, although not necessarily, react in some specific way, even if only by an effort not to show that I am suffering. To be in pain is to be disposed or inclined to react with some move-ment of avoidance, although the reaction may be inhibited at will. The feeling is inconceivable without the tendency to action, and the action is a natural expression of the feeling. Actions are performed in a certain way or in a certain spirit, which can be qualified adverbially. In retro-spect one may concentrate one's attention on that feature of the situation or action, which would normally be repre-sented by the adverb, or on that which would normally be represented by the verb. But the separation of 'features' here, which is achieved by reflection and guided by the forms of language, is not a separation of entities that have a clear and distinct identity. 'The same action performed in a different manner or in a different spirit'—the sense of sameness implied in 'same action' varies widely with the context and with the nature of our interest in speaking of it. I could regard the action as falling under a different heading, and classify it differently, because the impulse that prompted it was different, or because the style and manner of the performance was interestingly different. Certainly I do not naturally draw a line that bisects the action into the inner, unobservable feelings on the one side, and the publicly observable physical movements and perceptible expression and manner on the other side. And 'perceptible expression and manner' is a phrase that in itself shows that the bisecting line has not been effectively drawn. All human activities are to a greater or lesser degree performed in a certain style or manner, which is always taken to be a partly natural and partly conventional expression of the thought and impulses which accompany them. When we see a man acting, we normally see a whole performance in a standard social setting, not simply a set of physical movements. But the performance may be contrived to conceal feeling and intention, and we may not see through the performance to the feelings and intentions that in such a case will be said to lie 'behind' it. For the agent himself, there is always the possibility that he may not in fact do what he intended to do by some accident or miscalculation; or he may forget in the course of his action exactly what his intention was. But, while we are awake and fully conscious, we are all the time acting and moving with intent, and for much of the time our thinking is practical thinking, issuing directly in intended action and not formulated in words. I may learn of some misconception about the objects around me by a failure in trying to carry out my intentions. I may learn that my situation, including the relation of my body to objects around me, is in some respect different from what I had implicitly assumed that

78

it was. At all times I carry with me an unformulated assumption about where I am in relation to other objects, about the situation in which I am acting, thinking, planning, feeling, and this presumed situation constitutes the presumed point of view from which all other things are seen and interpreted. If I knew nothing of my true situation, I would be either mad or dreaming. In sane and waking life I may be deceived to some degree, for one of many possible reasons misidentifying the objects around me, including perhaps even some parts of my own body. But, sane and awake, I always have some direct and more or less precise knowledge of the position of some of my limbs and of some of the movements of my body, and these are as much parts and features of the 'external' world as is the distant clock and its movements. The mind animates, and enters into, the movements and reactions of a body that is in a sense one of these 'external' objects and in a sense is not 'external'; for this reason the use of the phrase 'the external world', in the philosophy of Russell and his successors, can be misleading. The pain that I feel, when an intentional movement of my arm brings me into violent contact with another object, is 'internal' in the sense that, unlike the movement of my arm, it is not something that is observed, and therefore not something that can be observed by different observers from different points of view. It is 'external', in the sense that it is localised in my arm together with the 'feel' of the object. The pain, no less than the feel or the look of the object, informs me of the object's existence in a particular place, as an obstruction to my movements. The use of the personal pronoun here, 'me', cannot be eliminated and replaced by 'my body', as if my body were an external instrument that I use. The obstruction is an obstruction of my action and not merely of my

79

body's movement; my plan is obstructed when my leg meets the obstructing object.

There is a common path of reasoning that starts from the fact that I may speak of my arm or of my leg, or of any part of my body, as an external instrument and that concludes that I may therefore speak of my body, taken as a whole, as an external instrument. This inference from parts to whole, which is more often implicit than explicit, is invalid. I may use my arms rather than my legs, my head rather than my shoulders, to bring about a certain effect or in performing a certain action. I may lose control, for one reason or another, of my arms and legs, and of my head and shoulders. They may then be thought of as instruments which I, distinguished from these instruments, suddenly find that I cannot use. But there is no equivalent sense in which I can be said to use my body, taken as a whole, in bringing about a certain effect or in performing a certain action; for there is scarcely a conceivable opposition between using my body, taken as a whole, and using something else, my mind. Certainly there is a vast variety of circumstances in which I may contrast my mind and my body; for example, I may contrast training my mind with training my body. In both cases *I* am being trained. The difficult and unnatural idea is that I might hesitate between using the two instruments at my disposal, my mind or my body, as I might hesitate between using my arms or my legs for a particular purpose. If a man is totally paralysed, and has lost the use of each and every one of his principal limbs and organs, it would still be unnatural to say that he had lost the use of his body and that he retained only the use of his mind. In fact it will never be true to say, in all strictness, that there is literally no bodily action which the supposed paralysed man can perform. Can he not hold his breath or avert his gaze? It is not altogether a contingent matter of fact that there will always be something in this range that he can do, while he is alive and conscious. A change of attention or intention must eventually embody itself in some movement of a sense-organ or in some act of communication, even if only in an arrested and imperfect form; even pure thought must have a possible issue. And we do not learn of this necessity only from medical science; for we would not call a man conscious if even his smallest movement was independent of his volition. There are circumstances in which I might wonder whether an arm or leg seen by me was my arm or leg; it does not follow that there could ever be circumstances in which I could wonder whether a body seen by me was my body. I could certainly wonder whether a reflection or representation was a reflection or representation of my body. But it is impossible that, pointing to some perceived object, I should ask 'Is this my body?' and not really mean 'Is this *part* of my body?' Pointing is essentially pointing *away* from myself, and one could give no sense to the idea of my body being at the other end of the pointing gesture, as my leg might be. I would be implying by my question that I was nowhere myself, a disembodied spirit; then there could be no meaningful gesture nor any other kind of indicating analogous to the act of pointing. A question that might arise about each and every one of the parts does not necessarily make sense when asked of the whole. It is a contingent, and not a necessary truth, that this or that particular part of my body has not been removed, physically separated from me. It is a necessary, and not a contingent, truth that my body has not been removed, physically separated from me. I am necessarily situated in the same place as my body, although it is possible to suppose any part of my body being detached from the whole. It is a condition of referring to anything, which is in turn a condition both of meaningful discourse and of meaningful action, that I should be able to point (in some way) away from myself. This makes it necessary that the gesture of pointing to myself, to 'here' must show in its physical pattern that it is reflexive, in the sense that it turns back to its point of issue. I may be uncertain in discriminating the objects that stand at the far end of the indicating gesture. But I cannot fail to indicate a being that points when I turn the gesture back on itself. This is the sense of the Cogito, the literal sense, which because it is a presupposition of the use of language, cannot be clearly expressed in language.

Even the totally paralysed man, whose only action is the directing of his own thoughts, may form the intention of turning his gaze in one direction rather than another, even if he consistently fails to achieve the result. He understands that he is seeing the world from this particular position and that his position determines the range of his possible action and observation. The position that he, and therefore his body, occupies is the base from which the sense of his referring words and the sense of his actions are directed outwards. Only in dreams do we seem to ourselves to move discontinuously from one scene to another like disembodied spirits. That we do dream is only a contingent fact of natural history, but it is one of those natural facts, like the particular conformation of our sense-organs, that are not easily thought away. The discontinuity between the successive standpoints of the dreamer in his dream may make it impossible to provide any true and consistent narrative of the dreamer's actions in the dream. Any account of a person's action requires that there should be some continuity between the intention and the effect; and that there should be a continuity in space between the agent's situation at the beginning of his action and at the end. Either he must be at the same place throughout the action or he must have moved through a series of adjacent positions. If he had *no* knowledge of his own situation, and was *wholly* deluded about his position as an object among other objects, we would be compelled to say that he was unconscious, because none of his actions would be directed to the objects around him and therefore he would have no intentions. Dreams have always been interesting to philosophers because they show the breakdown of these otherwise obvious and unavoidable conditions of human action and observation. The agent and observer becomes unconnected with a consistent world of objects, a transcendent observer, as Descartes imagines him, who, bodiless and outside any consistent scheme of things, sees impressions pass before him like a film. In constructing a narrative of his dream, his problem can only be to interpret this film of impressions and to ask himself what it represents. If his dream intentions are translated into effective action, this must seem accidental or magical; there is no reason in a dream-world why any particular intention should be followed by any particular result. In the Cartesian world also it is a divinely inspired accident that acts of will, issuing from a detached mind, are transformed into physical movements. To Descartes' question 'How can I ever be sure, beyond the possibility of error, that I am not dreaming?' one possible answer is that the consistent flow of intention into action, while I am awake, makes waking experience intrinsically unlike dream experience in exactly these respects. If a man, who showed some of the physical symptoms of awakening from sleep, also showed himself totally

83

unaware of his own situation in relation to other objects, we should have to say that he had not yet awakened and that he was in some kind of trance or dream. Even if after awakening from a dream I discovered that I had lost my memory and knew nothing of my own publicly testable past, I would still distinguish my waking experience from my dream experience, because the difference would show itself in the dissimilarity between the process of awakening and the process of falling into a dream or trance.

If I speak and think and act at all, even rather madly, there is necessarily a certain constancy in my references to myself and to my own present standpoint and to my separation from other objects, and, reciprocally connected with this, a certain continuity of self-consciousness as my intentions are translated into action. If I act upon things, I see myself as opposed to the external reality which I alter, even if I am deluded about the proper description of the things with which my action brings me in contact. If I were wholly deluded about the true nature of the things surrounding me, the effect of my actions would not coincide with my intentions, while the delusion lasted. That which I in fact did would not systematically coincide with that which I thought I was doing or meant to do. If I was totally deluded about the proper *description* of the objects around me, and systematically supposed things to be called something other than they were actually called, there would still be some consistency in my misuses of language while I was acting. If there was no consistency at all, it would be impossible to attribute any definite intention to me. My actions would become senseless and without direction and scarcely to be described as 'actions'. If I know what I am doing, I necessarily know something of my present situation, since any description that I would give of my action implies something about my present situation. If anyone else knows what I suppose myself to be doing, he necessarily knows something of what I believe my situation to be. This correlation must be stressed, because the flow of intention into action, the intention governing and directing action, requires a continuity of self-consciousness that may be forgotten if philosophers concentrate solely on our knowledge of the external world through the senses. Even if my memory totally fails, I still have this knowledge of my own recent history, and this means of distinguishing this one individual, myself, from the other particular things around me. To myself I am always a continuing thing producing changes, of which I know directly that I am the cause. The notion of a perceiving subject is also the notion of a continuing, embodied and intentional agent, who displaces, or is displaced by, the things around him.

However difficult it may be in speech to ensure that one is still understood to be referring to the same thing as before among the different things around one, the speaker can always make clear to what particular thing he is referring *now* by tracing the relation of the thing to himself at this particular moment. A person acting and speaking always has, therefore, a fixed base, or point of origin, to which any of his references to other things can at any time be traced back. He can without absurdity express doubt about the existence of any particular thing to which he is referring—'Is this a dagger that I see before me, or is it a figment of my imagination?' But no man can express a doubt that will be counted as a doubt about his own existence. Nor can he wonder whether he is himself a being who makes intentional references and performs intentional actions. If the point of origin is questioned, the application of the whole grid of thought to reality is questioned. Each of us, although using a common vocabulary, attaches his statements and questions to reality by the references that we make to things each from our own point of view. I may entertain the *possibility* of my being withdrawn from the world, of my not being here and of my never having existed. I may then consider what other things would have been different in consequence: 'supposing I did not exist, so-and-so would not be happening, and everything would be better'. But nothing would count as my believing that the condition stated in the protasis of this hypothetical proposition is true, and nothin would count as wondering whether it is true. When I in this way consider the difference that my existence has made, I am considering the effects of the existence in the world of a person having the properties that I have. The possibility of my not existing, as here considered, is the possibility of no one having had just these properties at this time and in this place. And plainly there is nothing self-defeating in this supposition. Nor is there anything self-defeating in the supposition of my lacking any one, or any set, of these properties. The absurdity arises only if I try categorically to deny my own existence, or try to attach sense to the question of whether I exist, while refusing any paraphrase of this question. It is not true that the absurdity of this behaviour lies only in the fact that the mere expression of the denial or of the question in itself seems to constitute an answer to it. The absurdity is more fundamental. I can intelligibly ask— 'Does this man, whom I seem to see before me, really exist?' even though the formulation of the question, with the words 'this man', may seem in itself to imply a positive answer. The answer might be—'No, there is nothing there: what you were referring to was only a figment of your imagination and not a man or any physical thing.' But the pronoun 'I', and the first person singular form in general, is more than just one more demonstrative device in language, parallel and on the same level with 'this' and 'that', and with the other personal pronouns. The first person singular is the nucleus on which all the other referential devices depend. Since each of us speaks and understands from his own point of view, we have to trace any spatial or temporal reference to, or from, here and now, which is our own particular standpoint. Any place referred to is at some definite distance from here, and any time referred to is traceable back to the point of origin, now. The final point of reference, by which a statement is attached to reality, is the speaker's reference to himself, as one thing, and one person, among others. Descartes assumed that a thinking being could without absurdity be conceived as existing alone and disembodied, at no particular place and no particular time. But my reference to myself in my own thought is a reference to something that indubitably points to itself and away from itself, and that directs its attention in one direction rather than another, and that sometimes changes its perceptions by its own actions. If this were not so, and if I could only be said to be the subject of a series of thoughts not directed towards any particular things, there could be no answer to the question—'Who am I? Am I the same person as the person who first thought so-and-so and then thought so-and-so?' If this question cannot be answered, there is no sense in saying that I think so-and-so, and nothing is then distinguished or picked out by the pronoun. 'I' would become a shorthand expression for 'whatever thinks'. If I am a thinking thing, there must be some criterion by which I can be distinguished from other actual or possible beings of the same kind. The criterion of

identity would have to be found in the thoughts themselves. But it must be logically possible for two people to
entertain the same thoughts in the same order, and, if so,
it is impossible to find any criterion of identity for thinking
beings among thoughts alone. One is therefore driven to
the conclusion that, when on reflection I find my own
existence indubitable, I am finding the existence of one
enduring thing of a particular kind indubitable, the thing
to which I am referring by the word 'I', and which can be
distinguished from other things of the same kind by its
position, the position that I suggest when I point to myself
and away from myself to other things. If I cannot doubt
my own existence here, I also cannot doubt that there
exist other things over there and away from myself, even
if I am doubtful, in a sceptical mood, about what they are
and how they are properly to be described. When I refer
to myself here, I implicitly contrast myself with other
things over there. If I were to say 'I cannot doubt that
I exist, but I can doubt whether anything else exists' I
might mean only that I cannot describe any other thing of
the existence of which I can be sure in the same way and to
the same degree as I can be sure of the existence of this
meaningfully pointing, doubting being that is myself.
Whether or not it is finally acceptable, this is at least a
superficially intelligible statement from a sceptical philosopher. But if the sceptical formula is interpreted to mean
—'I cannot doubt that I exist, but I cannot be sure, in the
same way and to the same degree, that I am not the only
existing thing in the world'—the statement, taken as a
whole, becomes unintelligible. When I refer to myself as
doing something and as active, even if the activity is only
that of directed thought, I make a contrast between that
which I myself do and that which happens to me, a contrast

that I would not understand unless something external to myself does sometimes impinge upon me.

For these reasons among others, no one has ever succeeded in stating a philosophical doctrine that could properly be called solipsism. We can be endlessly doubtful about the criteria of truth and sincerity in the communication of feeling. But I cannot doubt that there are in fact other thinking beings who present me with thoughts that were not originated by me and who refer to me as 'you' exactly as I refer to them, each of us perceiving the other from our own positions in space. I recognise meanings and intentions that are not my own in their gestures, words and actions. My assurance of my own position in the world, and my knowledge of other things, develops in this communication and could not conceivably develop except in this social context. To learn to speak and understand a language, as a child, is to enter into a set of social relationships in which my own intentions are continually understood and fulfilled by others and in which I encounter their corresponding intentions. I learn to describe and to think about things, and to think about my own actions, only because of this interchange and through the social conventions that constitute the use of a language.

Chapter 2

INTENTION AND ACTION

SPEAKING and writing, acts of communicating, are members of a group of actions of which gestures, the making of signs, the drawing of pictures, ritual movements, ceremonies of all kinds, are also members. 'Why did you smile?' 'Why did you wave your hand?' 'Why did you say that?' One can inquire into the reason for such actions, and into the intention that lies behind them on a particular occasion, no less than into the reasons for a blow or for an ordinary movement. It is necessary first to view the using of language as a particular kind of human behaviour, before viewing the forms and rules of language independently and for their own sake. Otherwise we may assume from the beginning too simple an opposition between speech and action and between thought and action, as so many philosophers have; and this will distort our later arguments about the nature of moral and aesthetic questions. If we are inclined to say that the domain of morality is the domain of action, how are we to mark that which is properly to be called an action for these purposes, and upon what principle? To make a statement, aloud and in the hearing of others, is certainly an action, and the nature of the action, as a specimen of human conduct, depends both upon the meaning of the statement and upon the circumstances in which it was made. But is a conclusion that I reach in my own thought, the assent that I give to a statement in my own mind, an action? Perhaps I ought not to have believed what I was told, and perhaps it was morally

wrong, and not only intellectually incompetent, to leap
to this discreditable conclusion. It would be a crude metaphysics that implied that an action is necessarily a physical
movement, or that I could not be seriously at fault in
viewing a problem in a certain way, in failing to concentrate, or in forming a certain opinion on certain data. It has
been part of the purpose of my argument so far to question
the naïve dualism that divides, within a person's history,
the internal and mental from the external and physical.
The concepts of thought and action, that is, of deliberate
human action, prevent any such separation being carried
through consistently. As soon as one realises that the using
of language, both in the practical calculation that may
accompany physical actions and in the making of statements, is itself a kind of behaviour interwoven with
other kinds, one is free to consider the range of essential human interests afresh and without prejudice. In particular one is free from the prejudice that the concept of
action itself is by itself sufficient to mark the domain of the
essential human virtues. One has before one, for reflection
and comment, whether in one's own person, or in the
person of another, always a whole person, including the
way he thinks and expresses his thoughts and feelings, the
things that he notices and neglects, the attitudes that he
adopts, the feelings that he restrains and the feelings to
which he allows free play, the words that he chooses to use
or that he uses unreflectingly, the gestures and physical
reactions that he controls or suppresses, the plans that he
makes and the sudden impulses that occur to him. All
these are features of the actions and reactions of a person,
upon which his own deliberation may be exercised, and
upon which his own judgment, or the judgment of others,
may pronounce. The distinctions that we may make

among these and other features of a person's life, by regarding some as ultimate ends and others as subordinate means, will be, at least in part, distinctions of value; in laying emphasis on some and neglecting others, we will be marking that which we ourselves believe to be essential in human life. It is philosophical self-deceit to pretend that the proper subjects for evaluation, and for the exercise of the will, are already marked out for us by an ordinary, undisputed concept of action. The ordinary concept of action, because it is a formal concept like 'event' and 'thing', must be altogether indeterminate. A philosophical inquiry is needed to decide what shall properly count in this context as action. As part of this philosophical inquiry, the moral question arises whether men's actions, however defined, are alone important, or whether thought and feelings are in themselves valuable apart from their expression in action.

It is a necessary condition of any human activity being regarded as a process of thought that it should involve the use of words, or of other symbols, in accordance with rules. But the thought that guides and accompanies deliberate action, and which constitutes intention, is not necessarily and always to be described as a *process* of thought, and does not necessarily always involve the use of words or of other symbols. There is a tendency in philosophy to represent the thought that guides and accompanies action as an adapted version of the process of thought of a mathematician solving a problem or of a scientist weighing evidence. These are always apt to be taken as examples of 'pure' thought, with the implication that other kinds of thought are more or less diluted versions of the pure. One possible sense of the word 'pure' here is only that the mathematician and the scientist, while engaged upon their problems, are doing nothing else but thinking; it is not that the thought is pure, but rather that the mathematician's or scientist's whole activity is thinking, unmixed with anything else. In this sense of 'pure', I am engaged in pure thought when I am sitting in a chair reviewing reasons for and against two courses of action open to me. Yet any thinking that is directed to a problem of this kind may be called impure, in another sense, simply because the object aimed at is not a statement but an action or a set of actions. We ordinarily associate thought mainly with an interest in truth and therefore with an interest in statements. But if we have also been persuaded that the making of statements, and the using of language, is properly to be viewed as a particular kind of behaviour, it is plain that the opposition between thought and action has been wholly confused. It is necessary to start again with new distinctions.

I shall assume that we can distinguish, in any activity on which we are engaged, the predominant point or purpose or end of that activity. At any time, when a man is awake and conscious, there is at least one, and generally more than one, answer that he would give to the question—'What are you doing?' I am not suggesting that it is a necessary truth that a man is always doing something active and purposeful, or that it is necessarily senseless for him to answer idiomatically 'I am doing nothing' or 'I am not doing anything in particular', when he is vacantly musing or resting. But it is a necessary truth—and one of the most important truisms about human beings—that, if a man has been fully conscious for some time, there must be some verbs of action that truthfully summarise what he has been doing during that time. The verbs of action may represent him as doing something desultory, purposeless and inactive. The mode of performance may vary through many degrees: but if conscious, then necessarily performing, and if unconscious, necessarily not performing, in the sense that no action is attributable to an unconscious man as its agent. It has been a mistake, common in empiricist philosophy, to represent human consciousness in waking life mainly as a state of passive awareness, as opposed to a state of unawareness of the external world in sleep and unconsciousness. A more decisive difference between consciousness and unconsciousness lies between the necessity of intended action in the one case and of mere natural movement without intention in the other. The sleeping and unconscious man is not an agent, and the effects of any movements that he may make cannot be related to his intentions. It is a necessary truth that he has no intentions under these conditions. Anything that can be said about him in a narrative covering the period of his unconsciousness—that he dreamt of so-and-so, that he called out a certain name, that he tried to raise himself and to walk— is so interpreted as not to attribute to him an action performed intentionally and at will.

Here it seems that the argument is going in a circle. I have argued that there is always and necessarily an answer to the question 'What was he doing?' asked about any man who was conscious at the time referred to. Why is there no answer to the same question asked about an unconscious man, except that in this case it is dogmatically asserted that the verb of action does not represent an action, in the full sense of an intentional action? An independent criterion of intentional action must be supplied, if the assertion of a necessary connection between consciousness and intended action is to have any force. A criterion may be sought in the way in which the question 'What are you doing?' is normally interpreted and answered. It seems to be characteristic of an intentional action that a man who accuses the agent of answering the question 'What are you doing?' wrongly accuses him either of deliberately lying, or of misdescribing his own activity in some more or less trivial way. It seems that he can never accuse him of simply not knowing what he is doing, of sheer ignorance in this respect, without implying that his action is not intentional. But the criterion is still not correctly stated. It is possible that a man might not in fact be doing what he honestly says that he is doing, without it being true that he is not doing what he intended to do. He might make a mistake in describing the achievement at which he was aiming, because he has false opinions about the proper and conventional description of the achievement intended. That which he honestly said that he was doing, when asked the question 'What are you doing?', might not be a correct account of what he actually intended to achieve. But still there is a logical connection between what a man knows or thinks that he is doing and what he intends to do. If a man is doing something without knowing that he is doing it, then it must be true that he is not doing it intentionally. Yet a man may be doing something intentionally in circumstances in which he may be said to have a false opinion about the nature of his intended action, in virtue of the fact that he honestly misdescribes it, or that he would misdescribe it, if the question were raised. What I actually intend to do is not necessarily the same as I would honestly say that I intend to do, if I were asked. I may very easily make a mistake in the description or identification of my activity as an activity of one kind rather than another without being confused in my practical intentions. That my intentions were clear in my own mind, even though I had expressed them wrongly in words, would be shown when I recognised something as happening contrary to my intentions, or recognised it as happening in accordance with them. I might say truthfully '*This is not what I intended*', even though I point to something that accords precisely with my own declaration of my intentions. My intention was not what I had declared it to be. But it does not follow from this that I did not know what I was doing, in one familiar sense of this treacherous phrase. 'Knowing what one is doing' may be used to mean the same as 'doing something with a clear intention to bring about a certain result' and not as equivalent to 'being able to give a correct account in words of what one is doing'. I may be trying to do something, and going forward with a fixed and definite intention in my mind, and still be liable to make a mistake of some kind in characterising my action into words.

There are very great complexities in the concept of intention, and not all of them are verbal ones, associated only with the particular idioms of the English language. They cannot all be unravelled at once, even if they can be finally unravelled at all. Yet nothing else in ethics and the philosophy of mind can be made comparatively clear unless this notion is comparatively clear. The notion of the will, of action, the relation of thought and action, the relation of a person's mind and body, the difference between observing a convention or rule and merely having a habit —all these problems find their meeting-place in the notion of intention. At this stage of the argument we need to distinguish the senses in which the questions 'What are you doing?' or 'What is he doing?' may be taken as inquiries into intentions. I may pause in the midst of some activity and ask myself the question 'What am I doing here?' having forgotten for the moment what my intention was, or, colloquially expressed, having forgotten what I was 'up to'. While we are fully conscious and in possession of all our faculties, this steady buzz of intentional activity continues, and we are to this extent necessarily and at all times in a position to answer the question 'What are you doing here?' or 'What are you doing now?', even though we had not previously formulated what we were doing in words. More often than not we have not previously expressed to ourselves our intention, or formulated it in words. But it is the *possibility* of our declaring, or expressing, our intentions from moment to moment, and if the question is asked, that gives sense to the notion of intention itself. Without this possibility, the notion of intention becomes empty. The question 'What is he doing?' when asked with reference to an animal is most easily taken simply as a request for a description of its overt activities, present and future and their regular effects, as these are visible to an observer. But the question is not in fact always so interpreted, because of the evident analogies between some kinds of animal behaviour and the purposive behaviour of human beings. A dog is seen scratching the ground, and to the question 'What is he doing?' a natural answer is 'He is looking for a mouse', or perhaps even 'He is playing at hunting a mouse'. Here it might seem that the intention behind the activity is being stated, because at least the point and purpose of the activity are stated. But the more intellectual word 'intention', since it is associated with the possibility of a declaration of intention, is out of place in the context of animal behaviour; the word 'purpose' certainly is not out of place. It is characteristic of an intention that it may be formed long in advance of the action intended, and also that an intention may have existed without ever having been translated into action. It is senseless to speak of what a dog intended to do before it was interrupted or prevented or changed its mind, unless 'He intended to do so-and-so next' is taken to mean the same as 'He would have done so-and-so next, if he had not been prevented'. To say of a person 'He intended to do so-and-so next' is certainly not equivalent to the statement that he would have done so-and-so if he had not been prevented. One might well believe that a person would have done so-and-so if he had not been prevented, and yet deny that, at the time referred to, he actually intended to do it. Conversely, one might believe that someone had seriously and sincerely intended to do something, and at the same time be very doubtful whether he would in fact have done it, or even have tried to do it, if and when the occasion for action occurred.

The difference here between a human being and an animal lies in the possibility of the human being expressing his intention and putting into words his intention to do so-and-so, for his own benefit or for the benefit of others. The difference is not merely that an animal in fact has no means of communicating, or of recording for itself, its intention, with the effect that no one can ever know what the intention was. It is a stronger difference, which is more correctly expressed as the senselessness of attributing intentions to an animal which has not the means to reflect upon, and to announce to itself or to others, its own future behaviour. The fact that the animal has no language, whether of words or of gestures, adequate to express its intentions is part of the sense of the conclusion that no intentions can be attributed to it. If we did attribute to a species of animal the power to speak a language, and therefore to make statements that are either true or false, we would be attributing to it the power to observe rules and conventions, and therefore the power to criticise itself as infringing the rules and the power to adapt its own habits to the rules. We would be supposing that it had passed from the state of nature into a civil society, with self-willed and adaptable institutions. It is not a fortunate accident, nor a detachable advantage, that men have a language adequate to express their intentions and that that which might otherwise have existed unknown, locked inside them, in fact becomes known. It is another aspect of the fact that they are social animals, capable of that kind of co-operation that is the observance of promulgated rules and of recognition of mistakes in the observance of the rules. Every convention or rule that I accept is an intention that I declare. Intentions are something that may be concealed and disguised; but they can be concealed and disguised, only because they naturally express themselves immediately either in words or in actions. The possibility of their finding an immediate natural expression both in words and in action is a condition of their existence. This connection of intention with language, and with the other conventional means of expression in society, ought to become clearer in a discussion of the intentionality of attitudes, states of mind and emotions. It would be senseless to attribute to an animal a memory that distinguished the order of events in the past, and it would be senseless to attribute to it an expectation of an order of events in the future. It does not have the concepts of order, or any concepts at all. An intention involves, among other things, a definite and expressible expectation of an order of events in the future, and is possible only in a being who is capable of at least the rudiments of conceptual thought.

Everyone has in his early life made the transition from a state of nature, without memory or rule, to a self-conscious existence as a social being. If it is impossible to ascribe intentions to animals, lacking the means either of expressing or entertaining even an elementary thought about their own future, it is equally impossible to ascribe them to infants, whose actions follow a more or less simple pattern of stimulus and response. Plainly there cannot be a hard and decisive line that marks the level of thought and co-operation, and therefore of powers of expression, at which it becomes possible to speak of a child having formed intentions that may or may not be translated into action. There is a large, blurred area within which it would neither be absurd to ascribe to a child intentions distinguishable from actions nor absurd to refuse to ascribe them. All hesitation is removed at the stage at which the child is able to make such statements as 'I shall do so-and-so after breakfast' or 'It was a mistake: I was not thinking what I was doing'. The fact that he is able to make such statements, or to make statements at all, justifies us in applying the distinction of intentional or unintentional to his actions, and in assuming that at any moment there are a number of things that he can truly be said to intend to do in the future, and also something that he can be truly said to be intentionally doing at the present, provided that he is conscious and therefore active. An intention is not a momentary occurrence, and the phrase 'at any moment' is only used to suggest that, as the permanent background of our waking life, we have at any time a number of changing intentions directed towards the future. So far from being momentary, to express an intention, or to impute an intention to do something to someone else, is in many ways like expressing or imputing a belief. I may have formed the intention or belief at a particular moment. Thereafter it can truly be said of me at any time that I believe so-and-so, or intend so-and-so, until I change my mind, even if I never give the matter another thought. My mind is made up about what I shall do, and remains made up unless for some reason I am induced to think again. Precisely the point of having a firm and fixed intention is that I do not need to think further about what I am to do, as the point of having a firm belief is that I do not need to trouble myself further to wonder whether a statement is true. Intentions, like beliefs, are not always and necessarily the outcome of a process of thought or of a datable act of decision. They may, like beliefs, effortlessly form themselves in my mind without conscious and controlled deliberation. When asked what I am going to do on a certain occasion in the future, I may find myself giving a definite answer without the least hesitation and without ever having reviewed the question before; this, I now recognise, had all along been my intention, just as I had all along believed without question that a certain statement is true. Any human mind is the locus of unquestioned and silently formed intentions and of unquestioned and silently formed beliefs.

A man's present intentions and his beliefs about his present situation and environment, taken together, constitute his present state of consciousness. His intentions obviously arise out of his beliefs about his situation and environment, and they must alter as these alter. He is attentive to, and forms beliefs about, those features of his situation that enter into his active interests and intentions. He sees reality around him, and his present situation, as a pattern of usable or obstructive things with which he has to cope, and he distinguishes and classifies things by their relation both to his permanent practical interests and to his immediate intentions. Therefore the questions 'What were you doing then?' or 'What are you doing now?' are the normal and natural way of inquiring about the man's situation at that particular time. His situation is defined by where he was and what he was trying to do. Even if he was unable to move, he would still answer the question with some statement of what he was doing at the time—perhaps 'listening to . . .' or 'looking at . . .' or 'thinking of . . .' He may succeed in disguising what he is trying to do, and he may make a mistake in describing and putting into words what he is trying to do. But there is a sense in which he unfailingly knows what he is trying to do, in contrast with an observer, simply because it is *his* intention and not anyone else's. There is no question or possibility of his not knowing, since doing something with intention, or intentionally, entails knowing what one is doing; and intending to do something on some future occasion entails already knowing what one will do, or at least try to do, on that occasion. There is therefore no need of the double, or reflexive, knowing which would be implied by the cumbrous phrase 'knowing what one intends'. To say 'I know now what I intend to do' is a redundant way of saying 'I know now what I shall do', and 'I know what my intention is in doing this' is an impossibly redundant way of saying 'I am doing this with intention or intentionally'. The only additional knowledge that could be required is the knowledge that such-and-such a form of words gives the correct description of what I am going to try to do, or of what I am now actually trying to do. I may very well be doubtful about this, and say 'I do not know, or I am not quite certain, whether this is the right way of expressing it or whether the thing I am trying to move is properly called a so-and-so or not'. But I cannot say 'I do not know whether I intend to move it'; and if I say 'I do not know whether I shall try to move it or not', the expression of ignorance is a disclaimer, honest or dishonest, of any formed intention. If my intentions are in this way unknown to me, then I have no fixed and formed intentions.

Philosophers, and particularly modern philosophers preoccupied with scientific knowledge, have turned attention away from the kind of thought and knowledge that is intentional and non-propositional, and that is not essentially expressed in testable statements. I may be certain, and announce that I am certain, about some future course of action of my own. The object about which I am certain is properly stated to be the action, and not a truth or a proposition about the action. How then—it may be asked —does the announcement 'I know now what I shall do to-morrow' essentially differ from 'I know now what will happen to-morrow'? Surely both are professions, or claims, of certainty about the future; the first about an impending action, which can also be regarded as an impending event, and the second about an impending event, but an event which is not directly connected with the will of the speaker? One may even suppose, in order to uncover the difference, that both sentences have been used by the same speaker referring to the same impending game or contest. In the first sentence he announces that he has now decided upon his own strategy in the game, and in the second—let it be assumed—he declares his confident belief about the course and outcome of the game, in which many players are involved. One difference between the two announcements of certainty is that the second of them provokes the questions—'How do you know what the outcome will be?' and 'How *can* you know?', where the first question is a demand for the source of the knowledge, and the second is a challenge to the claim to knowledge. No question either of the source of knowledge, or of the justification of the claim to know, can arise with a man's announcement that he knows what he is himself going to do in the game. He is not making a claim of any kind, but is rather declaring his intention and, in doing so, revealing that his mind is made up. Nor can there be any question of the source of his knowledge and of the means by which the knowledge was acquired. The difference appears more clearly when the form of words 'I know what I shall do tomorrow' is laid by the side of 'I know what he (or you) will do tomorrow'. The second sentence is normally used to make a claim that requires a justification and, as normally used, implies access to a reliable source of information; it is in these respects like the sentence 'I know what the outcome will be'. The first sentence, in the more usual of its possible uses, makes no such claim.

When this difference is admitted between the two kinds of knowledge, it must also be admitted that knowledge of the non-propositional kind is very familiar in speech. (1) 'I know what I want now'; 'I am not sure what I want': (2) 'I know what he wants now'; 'I am not sure what he wants'. These two pairs of sentences convey statements of knowledge or uncertainty, the first pair of the intentional and non-propositional kind, the second pair of the kind that is exposed to the challenges 'How do you know?' and 'How can you be certain?' The confession of an uncertainty of the second kind discloses lack of information and a need for further evidence. It shows ignorance upon a matter of fact, an ignorance that might be remedied by further inquiry into the evidence, or by further observation and testimony. A confession of an uncertainty of the first kind is not naturally described as a confession of ignorance, and even less does it disclose a need for further information and for an inquiry into the evidence. The transition from uncertainty about what (e.g. kind of food) I want now to knowing what I want is in many respects like a kind of decision. While I was uncertain what I wanted, and because I was uncertain, I was unable to answer the question 'What do you want?' If anyone else had claimed to know what I wanted, only my acceptance of his statement of what I wanted would finally substantiate his claim to knowledge. But the fact that I was uncertain does not necessarily imply that I did not want anything, or that there was nothing that I wanted, at that moment. Rather I did not know, because I could not identify, what I wanted. Similarly 'I do not yet know what I shall do' implies that any firm declaration of the form 'I shall do so-and-so', made at this moment, would be misleading and dishonest, since it implies that my mind is made up.

On the other hand there are important differences between knowing what one will do and knowing what one wants. First, coming to know what one will do is always and necessarily a case of making a decision and is not a case of making a discovery. Coming to know what one wants is partly a decision and partly a discovery, the proportions varying in different cases. If you claim to know what I will do, when I do not know myself, the expression of your alleged knowledge does not constitute direct help to me in the solution of my problem: for my problem requires a decision, and not a prediction. But your claim to know what I want, when I do not know myself, may solve my problem directly, and I may acknowledge that you are right: 'That is exactly what I want; how did you know, even better than I did myself?' A closer parallel in this respect can be found between knowing what one wants and the intention accompanying and guiding an action. Interrupted, I may forget what I came into the room for and not know what I am supposed (in my own original intention) to be doing. Someone else may supply the missing knowledge—'I know what you were doing'—and I might acknowledge that he is right, having recalled my original intention. A great variety of similar, and also slightly dissimilar, examples of intentional knowledge might be cited; knowing, and not being sure, what one likes; knowing, and not being sure, what one is frightened of; knowing, and not being sure, what one is hoping for. All these examples are bound together as examples of intentional knowledge, by the same difference between the forms 'I know what I . . .' and 'I know what you or he . . .', the difference emerging in the challenges that could be made to any announcement of the second form and that could not normally be made to any announcement of the first, autobiographical form. But the thought of an object that accompanies wanting and the thought of an object that accompanies states of mind and some kinds of feeling are in one important respect different from the practical thought that precedes and accompanies action. The thought that accompanies and precedes action is inextricably connected with the processes of deciding and trying. I may on occasion try to direct and restrain my desires and those feelings that are inseparably connected with the thought of an object. I will then be exercising my will, and trying to act upon my own desires and feelings. But the desires and feelings themselves are passions, not actions decided upon; typically, they occur, and are not chosen. I may be held responsible for them and for their direction if I do not decide, or do not try, to restrain or to change them when they are squalid and evil. But they are still the material upon which my will must act and are not themselves taken to be direct expressions of my will. I may make an attempt to change them; but they are not themselves attempts. All of them have some natural expression in action and forms of conduct, and they may be interpreted as themselves inhibited forms of behaviour: the feeling of anger is that which is left as a residue when the aggressive behaviour is controlled. Hence to control my anger comes to the same as to inhibit its natural expression. The feeling of anger remains as the passion when the expressive action, implied in the concept of anger, has been removed. It may be regrettable that I should feel pleased or sad or angry about something. But I have done all that I can do when I have restrained myself from behaving as a pleased or sad or angry man behaves, and when I have directed my thoughts appropriately. I may then cease to have those beliefs about the cause of my state which an angry man must have.

Of the many English verbs that centre upon the concept of the will, these verbs 'try' and 'attempt' are the most revealing and lie nearest to the centre of the concept. 'He is trying to do so-and-so' already states the agent's intention, with an added implication that there is some difficulty and a possibility of failure. The question 'What are you doing?' becomes the question 'What are you trying to do?' whenever difficulty or the chance of failure is stressed. The certainty about his own future action that a man enjoys when his mind is made up is the certainty about that which he will at least try to do, even if he is likely to fail. In order that he should attempt to bring about a certain effect, nothing else is required other than that he should have some idea of how the required result might be achieved and that he should make up his mind now. He can therefore be absolutely certain that he will try, merely in virtue of the fact that he has decided to try, even when he cannot be certain that he will succeed in his attempt. If he is asked the question 'Will you succeed?', he is asked to make a prediction, based upon the probabilities and the evidence of past successes and failures. If he is asked 'Will you try?' he is normally being asked for his decision and his intentions, and he is not being asked for a prediction; his questioner will not normally expect him to calculate the probability of his deciding to try. If he were asked to predict whether he will decide to try, when the moment for decision comes, he would normally do just as well, in satisfying the question, by making the decision immediately. In searching for a basis of confidence in his prediction, he will be led to identify the reasons that will incline his decision. There may be situations in which a man is asked to predict what his decisions will be, or what they would be in certain hypothetical conditions, and to predict without making a decision now. 'Under such-and-such conditions do you think that you, unlike me, would in fact try to rescue the man?' Here one is being asked to adopt a spectator's point of view towards oneself, and to judge how one will, or would in all probability, behave under certain conditions, in just the same way that one would calculate the probabilities of someone else's behaviour. It is only possible to ask this question in this form when the situation envisaged in the question is fairly remote from the actual situation of the person questioned. It would be pointless to require someone to predict his decision when the decision will in any case be made very soon. In addressing himself to the prediction he would reflect that he might just as well make the decision that he has been asked to predict. He would find himself in the situation of someone trying to predict something that is already beginning. The more remote the situation is from my actual situation, the more easily I can adopt a spectator's attitude towards

my own probable decisions and my own probable behaviour. The words 'Would you under these conditions try
to rescue the man?' would ordinarily be intended as asking
for a solution to a hypothetical practical problem, and as
hardly to be distinguished from 'What in your opinion
would be the right thing to do under these conditions?'
But the words might sometimes be used in the other
way, to ask—'Knowing yourself and your own tendencies
and record, what do you think you would in fact decide
to do?' Even if the contingency envisaged is remote, and
no real decision is called for, this question can scarcely
be answered in good faith. 'Knowing myself', in the sense
of knowing my tendencies and past record, is only a basis
for an answer on the assumption that I have decided, or
would decide, to acquiesce in these tendencies and that I
would not try to change them. I would be driven therefore towards making a hypothetical decision, towards a
choice of a course of conduct, rather than to making an
observer's guess of what my conduct would be. It is essential to human action, and it is a necessary condition of
human freedom, that it should be impossible that while I
am deciding what to do, and while I am therefore working
towards the state of being certain what I shall do, I should
at the same time ask myself the question—'Knowing myself
as I do, what am I in fact likely to do?' If I am undecided
about what I am going to do in some situation, and still
have no formed intentions, it necessarily follows that I am
still uncertain about what I am going to do. I might try to
end this uncertainty about the future by using ordinary
inductive methods, that is, by considering what I, and
other people similar to me, have in fact done, or attempted
to do, in similar situations in the past. I might reflect upon
the inclinations and impulses of which I am aware now, and

regarding them simply as the basis for a forecast, predict how I am likely to behave in the future. I might in this way succeed in bringing my uncertainty to an end; I might perhaps reach a conclusion about how I am likely to behave. But I could think about my own future action in this detached and inquiring way only at a time when no relevant practical decision was open to me. The 'could' here is a sign of a logical and not of a psychological barrier. Nothing would count and be interpreted as a detached observer's guess in a setting in which a practical decision was required from me. The short and sure method of ending the uncertainty, namely, actually deciding what to do, would be irresistible and unavoidable. If the uncertainty about my own future, an uncertainty that is logically inseparable from indecision, is an agony to me, I may also think that there is a shorter and more sure method of bringing it to an end: simply to decide to do one of the actions open to me, no matter which of them, without thinking any more about it. If I wish to avoid further uncertainty, I must wish to avoid further thought. But I do not normally put the question 'What shall I do?' to myself merely or mainly because I cannot bear the future to be uncertain. When the uncertainty about the future is painful to me, it is painful usually because it is an uncertainty about what will happen to me, about my fate rather than about my action. I wish to know what is likely to happen to me, in part at least because I wish to take some steps to avert the worst that is possible and to bring about the best that is possible. There seems therefore an absurdity in behaviour—an absurdity that is more than the infringement of a convention of language—in trying to find grounds for predicting what I myself will do. My inductive anticipations of the future are in general designed to serve my desires and intentions; for this reason they could not possibly replace them. I *first* need to use inductive methods to guess what will happen in the common order of nature and *then* to decide upon my own wilful intervention. I cannot—logically cannot—reverse this order, if I am to act deliberately and rationally at all. My attempts must be defined by my expectations of their effects. One cannot say what a man is trying to do unless one knows what he expects to happen. Expectation and decision are the two complementary aspects of the notion of action.

Why must my making up my mind to do so-and-so, which entails that I have become certain that I will try to do this, be distinguished from a prediction that I will in fact do it? The principal ground of the distinction seems to be a prior distinction, taken for granted in the use of ordinary language, between that which I myself do at will and that which happens to me. An attempt is by definition something that I do at will. Failure in the attempt is something that happens to me contrary to my intention whether the failure was culpable or not. Suppose that I decide to try to do something and at the same time decide, on the evidence of past performances, that I shall probably fail. It seems that I *cannot*, in the normal use of words, call the first decision a prediction and that I *must* call the second decision a belief, which, if it were expressed, would be called a prediction. If I call an expression of the first decision a prediction, I am thereby implying that the attempt will not be made of my own free will. If I deny that an announcement of the second decision is a prediction, I thereby imply that I am going to *make* myself fail, that is, that I will not, as I claim, really try. I may take steps which, from the point of view of an observer, may seem to be an attempt to do something; but they cannot be counted as a real attempt, if I have never had the least intention of achieving that which I seem to be aiming at. Can one be said to intend to achieve some result which one is all the time absolutely certain that one will fail to achieve? Scarcely. If I can be said to intend to achieve X, it must be true that I at least believe that there is *some* chance of my not failing in the attempt. I may sometimes take steps to achieve a result that I know to be impossible; the intention behind the attempt would then be to demonstrate the impossibility rather than to achieve the result. One may intelligibly say 'I have made up my mind to try, but I think I will probably fail'. But it is self-contradictory to say 'I will try, but I have made up my mind to fail'. Such trying would only be pretending to try.

It seems that the distinction between what a man does and what happens to him might be explained through the distinction between trying and not trying on the one hand and failing and succeeding on the other. It seems that I can always at least try to bring about a certain effect, even if, knowing myself and the circumstances, I am more or less certain that I will in fact fail. It seems that if I want to express my contribution to an action, and to distinguish this contribution from the external contingencies that may affect the total performance, I can always use the word 'try', distinguishing what I tried to do from what I actually succeeded in doing. Then 'I cannot now do so-and-so', in one of its uses, would be taken to be equivalent to 'I would not now succeed in doing so, even if I tried'. Any certainty that I may express about what I will or would try to do would be taken to express an intention and decision of mine. Any certainty that I may express about the outcome, about success or failure in the attempt, would be taken to be a prediction. Strictly speaking, I cannot decide to succeed and even less can I decide to fail. If I use the form of words 'I have decided to succeed in my attempt this time', I express only a mood of particular determination and confidence; an attempt in which I have decided to fail is not a serious attempt. Any certainty about my own future action, ambiguously expressed, would be settled in its sense by the question—'Are you telling us, and telling yourself, what you will try to do, or are you telling what will actually happen, that is, what the outcome will be?' As soon as the answer to this question is known, it is *eo ipso* clear whether a statement of intention or a prediction is intended.

Such a firm distinction would be convenient and clear. But it is not altogether well founded in the facts of normal discourse and in the way in which we generally think about human conduct. Why should I not tell you what I think I shall probably decide to do in a certain contingency and *refuse* to decide whether, in saying this, I am making a statement of intention or a prediction? What is the ultimate purpose and justification of insisting upon this distinction? The presupposition is that I must always distinguish clearly between my role as an agent and my role as a spectator, and as a spectator of myself among other things; and this is part of a deeper assumption that theoretical and practical questions must always be clearly distinguishable. Perhaps this last distinction cannot always be carried through. At least it must not be assumed in advance to be absolutely valid.

The unity of a person engaged in thinking, and in putting his conclusions into words, is certain, and does not need to be illustrated. One can always ask oneself, when one is perplexed or hesitant about something and is making some effort to think, why and to what end one is making this effort. Regarding any process of directed thinking, together with the effort that it sometimes involves, as one kind of activity among others, one may ask oneself—What was the point or purpose of this particular activity on this particular occasion? One might hope to find some distinction between theoretical and practical problems by considering the possible answers to this question and by finding that they fall into two distinct groups. Certainly a clear distinction cannot be found if, following some of the suggestions of Wittgenstein, one concentrates attention on the point or purpose of using a particular form of words, and considers thought principally as it emerges in utterances and in the social processes of communication. Then one will always be viewing the various forms of human thought through their natural expressions in language, predominantly therefore as social institutions and as types of behaviour in society. This is admittedly one side of human thought and, more than that, the social context of speech is the foundation and necessary pre-condition of any thought at all. It is inconceivable that there should be a form of thought that does not have its own natural and original expression in a particular form of communication, or in a particular form of behaviour. But there may be forms of thought which, once established through processes of communication, are cut off from their original source and which develop their own later and more sophisticated forms independently of any communication with others in a definite social situation. This is at least a possibility, which must not be prejudged. The point or purpose of *saying* something, in communication with others, may be persuasive, hortatory, informative, contractual in various degrees. The actual saying, the making of exactly this announcement at this time, is itself an action, for which there may be a variety of reasons, good and bad. I may have a purpose and an underlying intention, in *saying* 'I shall certainly do so-and-so', which are separate from, and additional to, the intention with which I first asked myself the question 'Shall I do it or not?' I may consider a theoretical question—e.g. whether a certain thing has a certain property—for practical reasons, or with a practical intention, and I may consider a practical question—e.g. what is the best way of bringing about a certain result? —with a theoretical interest. And I may have quite different motives and intentions in announcing my conclusions.

As philosophers, we generally wish to know whether there are two kinds of problem distinguished by the different patterns of argument appropriate to them, and which are such that we must approach them in our own thoughts with a different range of considerations in mind. When I am wondering what I shall do, I am certainly considering what would ordinarily be called a practical problem. But is it a practical problem, when I am wondering what I would do in some purely hypothetical circumstances? Or what I would have done if I had been in Mr Gladstone's position? Or what I would do if I were in your position? Must I in these cases decide whether I am considering what my behaviour would probably be, or whether I am rather considering what I would do, in the sense in which an announcement of what I would do would be a statement of intention or a declaration of policy? The answer is not obvious. The distinction between practical and theoretical questions is not already clearly drawn in our discourse. If it is to be introduced, one must first decide what purpose it is intended to serve.

To take the most simple situation first: I may sit down

to think what I shall do in an emergency demanding immediate action. Having reviewed alternatives and calculated the advantages and disdavantages, I act, my action constituting the solution of the problem that I actually adopt, whether or not I later regret it. Any man is continuously, and without interruption, responding to situations with actions that are to a greater or less degree deliberate and thoughtful. The sum of such acting, which may later be divided into separate individual actions in many different ways, constitutes his conduct or way of behaving during that period. He may also consider what he will or would do in contingencies that are remote in time or which are purely hypothetical and which may never in fact arise. Having thought, he may make a definite decision to act in a certain way, and thereafter can be said to intend to do whatever he has decided to do. The decision, which constitutes the solution of the problem considered, does not then appear for public comment, unless it happens to be announced. Unlike genuine actions, it is not there for all the world to see, but it still may be criticised later as a good or bad solution, as having been right or wrong. The decision taken in advance, and the intention formed for the future, are directed towards a situation envisaged or described, and not to an actual situation, a configuration of objects confronting the agent and perceived and distinguished by him. Therefore the problem that he solves is constituted by his own imaginings, or his own anticipatory descriptions, and it is to this extent an abstract and ideal problem. It presented itself to him in his own thought and was answered by him in his own thought. But it is not altogether clear what this answering, or solving of the problem, would consist in, if it was in no way related to an intention to act in a certain way. The solution of a practical problem that is not even indirectly connected with the possible action of the solver is a kind of shadow solution, without real weight or substance. We have this sense of trying to handle shadows when we are given 'examples' in text-books of moral philosophy. One should ask about any alleged solution— 'Would I really try to do this, and regret it if I did not try, or am I merely saying to myself that this is the right solution?' One further step towards the abstract and ideal, and away from the concrete, is taken when a man asks himself what he would do if a certain situation arose, where the situation is specified entirely in terms of his description of it and is not identified by any time or date at which it is supposed to occur. An answer to such a question would scarcely count as the statement of an intention, because the answer carries no definite commitment of a person to act in a particular way at a particular time; it would only count as a statement of intention if a speaker announced that he would *always* behave in such-and-such a way when the situation confronting him was of a certain specified kind. He would then be committing himself to a general policy of ignoring, as far as his own action is concerned, all other features of situations, whenever the mentioned features occur.

But if I am giving advice, and telling you what I would do in some situation confronting you, or if I am recommending a general policy of action to you in the form of words—'I would myself always be ruthless with people of that kind': or if I am considering some past behaviour of my own, and say 'If I had the choice over again, I would do exactly the same', I would not normally be taken to be declaring my intentions. Yet it seems certain that the kind of argument and reasoning that would be relevant to any one of these conclusions would be relevant to any of the others. There seems no difference in principle between the considerations that I would adduce if any one of these judgments were challenged, although some of them could be taken as statements of intention and some could not. The difference of principle comes in with the certainty or belief about my own future action, with the certainty that constitutes decision and the belief that constitutes intention. I may consider abstract possibilities, and I may guess how I would myself act if they were realised, and I may recommend policies of action to others. But I do not thereby profess any certainty about the future. Or I may consider my own past, or the past actions of others, and suggest to myself or to others alternative actions in those concrete situations. But there is no commitment, because there is no profession or certainty about the future. The commitment and the acknowledged certainty about my own future are two aspects of the same thing. I am committed in my own mind to act in a certain way if I have made up my mind so to act and if no doubt is left in my mind. This commitment is the shadow of the genuine social commitment that comes with a declaration of intention. If I had always said to myself that I would never do so-and-so, I would be ashamed of my self-deceit if in the end I actually did it. Self-deceit is a familiar shadow of social deceit.

A practical question might be defined, widely, as a question about what action is, was, or would be the right action in certain specified circumstances, actual or imaginary, and, more narrowly, as a call to someone to decide, when his decision is his certainty about his own future action. There is nothing in the human situation or in ordinary language that unavoidably imposes either definition on us. It is only important that the two senses should be distinguished, if the contrast between practical and theoretical questions is to be put to any use in philosophy.

We have so far represented human consciousness as the sense of oneself as one active thing among other things in a particular situation in the world, viewing the world from a particular standpoint and classifying the objects around one as instruments which one may use and which may obstruct and resist one's purposes. We have seen consciousness as inseparable from action, or attempted action, in the sense that we are always able to answer the question—'What are you doing now?'—as there is always an answer to the question 'Where are you now?' A conscious mind is always and necessarily envisaging possibilities of action, of finding means towards ends, as a body is always and necessarily occupying a certain position. To be a conscious human being, and therefore a thinking being, is to have intentions or plans, to be trying to bring about a certain effect. We are therefore always actively following what is happening now as leading into what is to happen next. Because intentional action is ineliminable from our notion of experience, so also is temporal order. It is important that we are capable of a type of experience, aesthetic experience, in which thought of the possibility of action is for a time partly suspended. The recognised value of aesthetic experience is partly a sense of rest from intention, of not needing to look through this particular object to its possible uses. This type of 'pure' experience, when it exceptionally occurs, does in fact give a sense of timelessness, just because it is contemplation which is as far as possible divorced from the possibility of action. In aesthetic experience I am not moving towards the solution of a problem, or choosing between alternatives, as I am in thought and action.

It is a characteristic of a question about the truth or falsity of a statement, outside pure mathematics, that it allows of a suspended 'Yes-and-no' answer, when the terms in which it is put do not precisely fit the reality. But a practical question, as narrowly defined, is posed by a situation that unavoidably demands a decision. The situation confronts me, and I shall unavoidably act in one way or another in this situation. To decide to do something is not the same as to decide to act in such a way as to satisfy a certain verbal formula. If someone says to me 'Have you decided to steal this thing?', and if I am very doubtful whether taking it would constitute stealing, it does not follow that I am doubtful about, and have not made up my mind about, what I am going to do. I may know exactly what I am going to do, even though I do not know whether what I am going to do is properly to be described as borrowing or stealing. Similarly, if I say: 'I have made up my mind about one thing: I shall act courageously this time', you may ask 'But have you made up your mind? What are you going to do?' And I may be compelled to admit that I have not. This is only the reverse aspect of the truth, already mentioned, that if I intend to do something, I infallibly know that I intend to do it, although I am not infallible in putting into words what it is that I intend to do. I may recognise that I have done what I intended to do independently of recognising whether or not I have done what I honestly said that I was going to do; I might not have succeeded in saying what I meant. It has been generally recognised in recent philosophy that the relation of words and statements to facts is elusive and can never be stated in any simple and general terms. It has not been so generally recognised that the relation between words and actions is equally elusive, and that there are the same difficulties in dividing a human being's conduct into a set of namable actions as there are in dividing the perceived world into a set of namable facts. Just as I am inclined to say, when I am told that I must have characterised my desires wrongly, 'I know what I want, even if I have used the wrong words in identifying it', so I am inclined to say, when told that I must have described my action wrongly, 'I know what I am trying to do, even if I have used the wrong words in saying what I am trying to do'. In both cases I am inclined to say 'I know, if anyone does, since I am the person concerned;' but knowing is here not the same as being able to put it into words correctly, which is an independent skill. Similarly I may say 'I know what you are trying to do', which does not necessarily imply that I can correctly describe what you are trying to do any more than 'I know exactly what you are feeling, as I have felt it myself' necessarily implies that I can describe what you are feeling. If I know what you are trying to do, I shall be able to point to the outcome of your activity and say 'This is, or is not, part of what you were trying to achieve', even though I was at first unable to describe correctly the achievement aimed at. English idiom cannot be confidently relied upon to mark the distinction between verbalised and unverbalised knowledge, since the English language, like any other, is often used carelessly. But one might try to mark the distinction as falling between 'knowing what I am doing' and 'knowing what it is that I am doing', where only the second claim is decisively rebutted if I fail to answer correctly the question: 'What are you doing?' There is the same difference between the phrases 'knowing what I, or you, feel' and 'knowing what it is that I or you feel'. 'I do not know what I feel' normally signifies that my feelings are confused: 'I do not know what I am trying to do' normally signifies that my intentions are confused. My feelings may be confused, in the sense that they fall into no stable pattern that I recognise from the past, as shifting colours may be confused before my eyes. 'I do not know what it is that I am feeling' (e.g. disappointment or jealousy or anger) normally signifies a difficulty only in classifying, as 'I do not know what it is that I am doing' (e.g. what this move in the game or craft is called), and often signifies an ignorance of the name or correct description. Analogously, but also differently, 'I do not know what I want' normally signifies confused desires, while 'I do not know what it is that I want' very often signifies an inability to identify the object of a desire that is in itself definite. There are many shades of difference, and a variety in the kinds of knowledge, that we may claim of our own attitudes, states and intentions; and there are many different shades of confusion and definiteness in self-knowledge. But it is an overriding truth that deciding what I want, like deciding what I am going to do, is distinguishable from finding the correct words to say or express what I want.

It may still be objected that if I have decided what I am going to do, it must be possible for me to state *roughly* what it is that I am going to do, even if I am unable to be entirely accurate in my statement. This is in general true, and particularly true of those who are competent in the use of language and who are accustomed to think in words. It is inconceivable that a man who knows a language, and who also knows what he is going to do, should sincerely give an *entirely false* account of what he is going to do, unless he has changed his mind between making his statement and taking action. If there is in general some recognisable correspondence between facts and his factual statements, there must be a similar correspondence between his actions and his declarations of intention. We otherwise will accuse him of systematic insincerity or self-deceit or, in an extreme case, of confusing an intention with a mere wish or hope. But I may have a highly detailed and specific plan of action about which I am unable to be specific in words, because I do not know the correct words. Or I may have a firmly fixed intention that does not involve a highly specific plan, but is rather an intention to do one or other of a particular range of actions; it may be my intention to rely on the circumstances to determine which of them I shall actually do. Intentions may in themselves be specific or vague, apart from the statement of them, which in its turn may be more or less specific in relation to the intention stated. No sense can be given to the idea of an absolutely specific intention, any more than to an absolutely simple fact. As there are no atomic facts, so there are no atomic actions. One may say, colloquially, that one had intended to do everything that one had in fact done, and that nothing in one's actual performance was either unintended or unplanned. This phrase is ordinarily understood, not with philosophical literalness, but against a conventional background of the classification of action. It implies that everything worth mentioning in the performance was intended and planned, and not that everything that could conceivably be mentioned by any verb of action was intended and planned.

My intention to do something is a settled belief about my future action, a belief that illumines some part of the future, like a beam of light with a periphery of darkness, the periphery not being clearly marked. There is something that I particularly had in mind to do in the centre of the beam, and on either side are by-products and accompaniments, more or less clearly thought of and intended, around the central intention. When I am asked the always answerable question 'What are you doing now?', I pick out the centre of my active intention of the moment, and therefore the centre of my consciousness; this is what I am, for the moment, absorbed in. Generally my active intentions, and therefore my consciousness, are turned towards the external world—'I am trying to move the table' or 'I am trying to find my watch'. The force of the metaphor of the 'external' world is that it includes everything that occurs among the objects of my active intentions. outside the lighthouse that illumines them for a moment. Not only my own body and its limbs may be seen as instruments and obstructions to my purposes, but also my own states of mind, moods and inclinations. They may seem to stand in the way of my purposes and my will, and to be in this sense factors in the order of Nature, to be reckoned with and circumvented. So it might be that my active intentions were turned inwards upon myself, and that I could truly answer 'I am trying to control my anger' or 'I am trying to make up my mind what I shall do this afternoon'. These sophisticated forms of speech represent a type of self-consciousness that develops only as the forms of language develop. I could not be doing, or trying to do, these things unless I had the means of saying that I was doing them. They become actions because I can think of them and represent them to myself as actions. I could be aware of a physical object, such as a table, and be trying to deal with it as an obstruction to my purposes, without being aware of it as a table, in the sense of knowing what it is and what is the correct description of it. But if I am aware of my own anger or fear, I must be aware of them *as* anger or fear, and therefore as tendencies to behave in a certain way, tendencies that I may decide to control. The metaphor of 'making myself', or 'bringing myself', makes it possible that I should conceive my feelings, otherwise inchoate, by analogy with a struggle with some material obstruction. It is only because I can speak metaphorically of 'watching' my own mental states, my impulses and inclinations, that I can also have the idea of bringing myself to, or making myself, do things. I can only be in a position to watch my own mental states, as opposed to simply having them or living through them, if I have the means of labelling them. Then I may think and speak of them as if they were objects to be manipulated in relation to my intentions. If I have formed the intention of entering the water, I may find myself confronting an obstacle that is not a physical object in my path. I may be aware of it as something within myself, which I may therefore try to remove or overcome, as I would try to remove or overcome a physical object. In metaphorical terms, my intentions, like a torch throwing its light forward, illuminate resisting objects in their path. I notice and single out from the chaos of reality anything that obstructs and that needs to be manipulated, identifying objects as things of a certain kind by their kind of resistance and manœuvrability in the face of my ordinary intentions. With self-consciousness and the resources of language growing together, and indissolubly together, men have developed a vocabulary for classifying also their states of mind by their tendencies to resist their will or as instruments for their purposes. The centre, from which everything else can be regarded as an object, is my will as an agent forming intentions and making decisions. I am carried forward from one moment to the next by my intentions, succeeding and failing in my attempts as my projects meet resisting objects.

British empiricists since Hume have tried, to their own dissatisfaction, to represent the known continuity of a person's consciousness as some binding thread of memory running through the separate data of consciousness. But within the trajectory of an action, with its guiding intention, there is already a continuity through change, and, if it is true that a conscious person is necessarily engaged upon some action, however trivial, this known continuity is interrupted only by sleep and by other forms of unconsciousness. It is not easy to state clearly what is meant by such phrases as 'the sense of my own identity'. But we can find in the reflexive idioms that we use in speaking of our own actions and intentions a kind of justification for such phrases. I do distinguish myself, as the inner core that is the source of directed effort, from all my passing states, and it is this sense of myself as the source of meaningful action that gives me the sense of my continuity from the present into the future. The sense of continuity is reflected in the absolute certainty that I can claim, when interrupted in the middle of an action, both about what I have just done and about what I am going to do next. Then the immediate future, as far as my own activity is concerned, can be as certain and fixed in my own mind as the immediate past. 'What are you going to do next?' 'I am going to try to lift that clock.' 'How do you know that you will try to lift it?' Or 'Are you sure that you will try?' 'You *must* be suggesting that I shall change my mind; for nothing would count as my not being sure, or doubting, that I am going to try, except my changing my intentions, or thinking again about the action.' If the speaker had been forcibly restrained in his action, and were then asked what he would have done next if he had not been stopped, he could claim absolute certainty about the truth of the quasi-hypothetical statement 'I was going to try to lift the clock, if I had not been stopped at that moment'. He could claim absolute certainty, merely in virtue of the fact that that was how his mind was made up. If an attempt and not an achievement is in question, nothing beyond the agent's decision is required in order to determine his future.

It is sometimes suggested that the past is necessarily that which is fixed and unalterable, and which therefore can be the object of certain knowledge, while the future is that which is necessarily unfixed and alterable, and which therefore can never be the object of certain knowledge. The second of these philosophical claims is not supported by evidence of the natural forms of speech. 'Certainly I shall try to come' is contrasted with 'I may or may not come: I do not know', exactly as 'Certainly I did that' is contrasted with 'I may or may not have done that: I do not know'. If it is suggested that I can never be absolutely certain about my future action, even the immediate future, because I may always change my mind, there is the parallel possibility that contrary evidence may appear to change my mind about the past. 'I am sure that I did do it' and 'I am sure that I will do it' are equally exposed to the objection 'You have said that before, and then changed your mind'. If the objection is pressed further—'But something might happen at any moment in the future to make me change my mind', the same can be said about the past; something might happen at any moment (perhaps new testimony from others) to change my mind about the past. Something altogether unexpected might happen which would constitute evidence leading me to change my mind about what I had actually done, or tried to do. And very often this suggestion that something might happen to change my mind would seem equally absurd for the future as for the past; as my memory is finally tested and clear, so also my intention may be finally tested and clear and all possibilities may have been considered. 'If I am not certain of this, e.g. that I will not try to murder him', I may say, 'I am not certain of anything'. But, it will be objected, the suggestion that something may happen to change my mind about the past is necessarily the suggestion that something may happen *in the future*, that new evidence *will* appear. This is certainly true. But it does not follow that my determination to act in a certain way must always yield a lesser certainty than my conviction, based on memory, that I did in the past act in a certain way. Plainly memory and intention, as sources of non-inferential knowledge, are limited in their range in different ways. I can only claim directly to remember a happening at which I was present and which I in some way observed, and I can only claim to know, as a result of a decision or formed intention, what I shall myself try to do. Any other knowledge of the future, like any other knowledge of the past, for which I may claim certainty, must be justified as an inductive inference based upon some general proposition, which has been thoroughly tested and found to be true in all examined cases. The knowledge of the future, which is my own intention to act in a certain way, is in no way an inference. Even if I declare my firm determination *always* to try to act in a certain way whenever certain circumstances arise, and if I am asked whether I am sure that I *always* will, I may answer: 'Yes: precisely this uniformity, this "always", is what I am determined upon.' The kind of reasons that I would give for making up my mind always to act in a certain way would be the basis of my certainty that I would always try to act in that way, provided that I thought that they were overwhelmingly strong reasons, which could never be outweighed in my mind by any other considerations. I might justifiably claim that it is certain that I will never try to murder someone, on the grounds that, being the kind of person that I am and leading the kind of life that I do, it is certain that nothing will ever happen to me which I would consider a sufficient reason for committing murder. This would be a complicated and ambiguous judgment. That nothing of a certain specified kind will ever happen to me, and that I will never confront a situation of a certain specified kind, I could only know by induction and from general experience of the world. But that nothing that I would consider a sufficient reason for murder will ever happen to me could not be taken as only and wholly a prediction, because, in saying what I would count as a sufficient reason for murder, I must be announcing a policy of action. I cannot avoid deciding for myself what I shall count as a sufficient reason for an action, and therefore I cannot represent 'finding' something a sufficient reason as something that happens to me, as a mere event in my consciousness. I do not helplessly encounter reasons for action; I acknowledge certain things as reasons for action. I can predict that something will occur that will tempt me to act in a certain way; so far I am surveying and foreseeing the common order of Nature. But I cannot in good faith predict that I will succumb to the temptation, unless I represent the temptation as altogether irresistible, and therefore as something more than a temptation. I cannot naturally represent my certainty that I will never find a sufficient reason to do something as based on my observation of the world, including myself as part of the world and my past decisions as events in the world. The principle here is that no one can—logically can—regard his past intentions as a basis for predicting his future intentions. The very notion of predicting what plans I shall form collapses into self-contradiction. Either I take into consideration the reasons that will influence me, in which case I am already engaged in forming a plan; or I somehow contrive to ignore the factors that will influence me, in which case I cannot honestly profess any confidence in my own prediction. If anyone says 'I expect I shall try to do so-and-so, because I always have tried in the past', he cannot disguise, by using this elusive form of words, his unavoidable freedom of action. He cannot make the 'because' here the sign of an inductive inference, parallel to 'I expect that he will try to do so-and-so, because he has always tried in the past'. That which he quotes as the basis or ground of his certainty that he will try to do so-and-so will be taken as his reason for doing it, if the doing is to be genuinely an action of his. If therefore he gives his past attempts as the ground of his confidence that he will make similar attempts in the future, he will be taken to be saying that the fact that he has done these things, or that he has made these attempts in the past, constitutes a good reason for doing, or trying to do, the same thing in the future. It may be true that men commonly do *say* 'I expect that I shall try to do this, because I always have in the past'. Men may say anything in self-deceit or from carelessness, without a firm awareness of the implications of their words.

But once again it may be objected that this discussion goes round in a circle. Tying the notion of action and of a reason for action together, and contrasting this pair with future happening and evidence for this happening, we say that any confident prediction of a future action by the agent is a declaration of intention, to be supported by reasons for action, and any prediction of a happening involving the agent is an inductive inference, to be supported by evidence. Even if it is admitted that these terms are properly tied together in this way to form two kinds of announcement of a person's future, what is the criterion that distinguishes one kind of utterance about a person's future from the other? Which of these distinctions—action as opposed to happening, reason as opposed to evidence—is to be taken as fundamental?

We have so far taken as fundamental and unanalysed the notion of intention, and the associated notion of an action as an attempt, as a trying, to achieve some result: as if it were evident when some change in the world could be said to be the intended action of the person involved and when it could be said to be a happening, and not an action of any person or persons involved. And the difference *is* in general evident in our experience, but evident on any particular occasion only to the person to whom the intended action, or attempt, is rightly or wrongly imputed. Consciousness is consciousness of intention. What I do, in the sense of try to do, I necessarily know that I do, in that use of 'know', already described, in which 'knowing' does not necessarily imply 'being able to state correctly'. Others do not necessarily know what I am trying to do, and when they do justifiably claim to know, they still cannot impute ignorance of my intentions to me, even though they can accuse me of dishonesty, or of various kinds of error in putting my intentions into words. They have only seen or heard, or otherwise perceived or inferred, what I am trying to do. I have never perceived or inferred what I am trying to do; I have always and unavoidably known. If being psycho-analysed I am led to acknowledge that I have for years been unconsciously trying to do so-and-so, but not consciously trying, this bringing into consciousness of a policy that was unconscious makes me thereafter, and for the first time, an intentional agent in this domain of my conduct.

Freud has given powerful, almost irresistible, reasons for speaking of unconscious policies and purposes as commonplace facts of human life. There are circumstances in which a man may be said to be pursuing a policy, and executing a plan, without in any sense knowing that that is what he is doing. He is powerless to control and direct these policies until he is brought to realise what he is doing; until this moment of realisation, his actions have a meaning and direction, clearly grasped by his analyst, which the agent has not himself given to them. If I needed to be told what I was doing, and if someone knew better than I did, it follows that I was not an intentional agent in the full sense postulated; only with knowledge comes the opportunity of choice and therefore full responsibility. If I did not know what I was trying to do, no possibilities of deliberate change were open to me. The knowledge of what I am trying to do is always and necessarily knowledge that I am going in one direction rather than another. The recognition of my own situation, of which my own unconscious wishes may be part, leaves me with a now unavoidable choice of policies. I can now look back on my unconscious purposes as something that happened to me, and perhaps is still happening to me, and the problem before me now is whether I can control these now recognised tendencies in my own conduct.

This may still seem a too comfortable separation of the conscious mind, as the seat of personality with which I identify myself, from the unconscious mind. Why should that which I knowingly do alone constitute that which I really do? Freud claimed that the processes of repression, inhibition and of resistance to analysis rather show the unity of the mind and of the personality in its two divisions. I am not, and do not feel at the moment of realisation, dissociated from the unconscious processes of my mind, when I am brought to realise them, as I do from physiological processes. I rather see in them my real character, and I am brought to acknowledge that I have not been, and perhaps am not still, wholly in control of my own mind and purposes. The realisation sets me free to control, or at least to try to modify, unconscious intentions, as awareness of my passions as being of a certain kind sets me free to control and direct their natural expressions. There is no contradiction or conceptual confusion in the phrase 'unconscious purposes'. The confusion arises only if intention is separated from consciousness.

To show the connection between knowledge of various degrees and freedom of various degrees is the principal purpose of this book. 'Why should that which I do with full knowledge of what I am doing alone constitute that which I do with full freedom?'—this question will only be answered by the whole argument. My own conscious intentions are, before all other things, present to me as a form of knowledge and constitute the centre of my consciousness at any particular moment. Intention is the centre, because at least part of that which I can be said to have noticed, or been aware of, at any particular moment follows directly from a statement of what I was trying to do at that moment. Admittedly it would be intelligible to claim that I noticed or was aware of some fact, or of some thing, that was totally irrelevant to what I was trying to do. My consciousness was to this degree divided and my intentions at that moment were not simple. Perhaps I was both listening to the music and trying to find something that I had lost. But it would be unintelligible to claim that I had not noticed, or was not aware of, something that I had already mentioned in stating my intention, although I might not have noticed *that* it was a thing of a certain kind and I might not have been aware of some fact about it.

We can now say that the concept of intention has at least the following features and connections with other concepts:

(1) The subject cannot be ignorant of his intention, although he may make a variety of mistakes in stating it, in putting it into words.

(2) To try to do something is necessarily to intend to do it, or to intend to come as near as possible to the achievement in view.

(3) To decide to do something is necessarily to form the intention of doing it.

(4) To intend to do something in the future is necessarily to believe that I shall in fact try to do it.

(5) To intend something to happen (as the result of my activity) is at the least to believe that it may and could happen. It would be self-contradictory to say 'I intend that to happen, but I am sure that it will not', or 'I believe that it is impossible'. But I may attempt something that I know or believe to be impossible, e.g., in order to demonstrate its impossibility or to test my powers. I may expect to fail, but I do not intend to fail, if I am seriously making the attempt. If, in response to a challenge, I try to run a hundred yards in eight seconds, and seriously try, my intention is to run as fast as I can and to approach the achievement as nearly as possible.

(6) At any moment of my waking life, there are always

things that I intend to do in the future and there are always things that I am doing with intention at that moment. It is also true that there are always things that I intend to happen. It follows that at any moment there are always things that are happening either in accordance with my intentions or contrary to them.

(7) In any use of language with a view to communication, whether in speaking or writing, there is an intention behind the words actually used, namely, that which I intend to convey, or to be understood, by the words used.

Someone may always inquire into what I at the time actually intended by the words that I used, apart from inquiring into the meaning that ought properly to be assigned to them in view of the established conventions of the language. Wherever conventional symbols of any kind are used, one may inquire into the interpretation intended by a particular person on a particular occasion, apart from inquiring into the correct interpretation prescribed by the conventions. The often quoted fact that human beings are essentially thinking, and therefore symbol-using, animals is a special case of the fact that they are essentially intentional animals. It is logically impossible that there should be beings who have a means of communication, properly to be described as a language, and who can be said to make statements to each other, but who do not act with intention. If we refuse to describe and explain the behaviour of a creature in terms of its intentions, we cannot describe its signalling system, and its method of communicating with other creatures, as the making of statements. The notion of a statement involves the notion of what the speaker intended to be understood. It is not enough that an utterance or signal should have an evident function, or serve a purpose, if it is to be classified as the use of a language. If there is a use of a language, there must be the intention to follow a convention or rule.

There has been confusion in modern philosophy because the intention behind a particular act of speech, or behind the act of writing down a statement or order on this occasion, may seem scarcely distinguishable from the intentions with which the particular words were chosen and used. Yet the question 'Did you, in saying that, intend to influence him?' is plainly a different kind of question from 'Did you, when you said that, intend this word to be understood in its older sense or in its modern sense?' The first question relates to the sense of the *action* of making that particular statement at that time, the second relates to the sense attached to the words. The interesting difference here is that the intention animating this particular action of speaking upon this subject at this time may vary widely. There are many different possibilities, widely various things that you might have meant to achieve by making exactly that statement at that time. Anyone interpreting, and trying to understand, your action will have to judge, on the evidence or from your testimony, what your intention in making that statement was. If the question is: 'How did he intend this word to be understood?' the range of possibilities open must ordinarily be very narrow. He could not (logically) have meant it to be understood in a way in which he knew that no one would in fact understand it; this would be the same as to intend that he should be misunderstood. He could not (logically could not) *make* the word mean in his own mind, or to him, something that he knows that it does not mean, by rule or custom. If this feat was possible, it would be no more than thinking of something else while uttering the word. If I use a word, or conventional symbol, seriously meaning something by it, it must be true that I expect it so be understood in a certain way, and that I believe that the recognised rules governing its use allow it to be understood in the way that I intend. The meaning or intention that animates the use of a symbol is in this respect different from the intention that animates an ordinary action of any kind. An action may indeed have an intention behind it, a sense, that is entirely contrary to its ordinary and recognised sense. I may make certain movements that are ordinarily a sure sign that I am trying to achieve so-and-so, while in fact I have a quite different aim in view. For this reason I can pretend to be going to do something, or I can give the appearance of doing it, when in fact my intentions are exactly the opposite. Among the actions that I can perform with an abnormal intention is the action of stating something—that is, I can lie. But I cannot (logically cannot) pretend to mean something by a certain word that I do not mean. I can say 'I shall come', without having any intention of coming and therefore 'without meaning it'. But I have not then meant something different by the *words*. On the contrary, I meant to deceive you by using exactly those words with their ordinary meaning.

There are very complicated relations between the intention with which I habitually say or write something on a particular occasion, and my intention that the words used should be understood in a certain way. These relations have been unhappily oversimplified, with serious consequences in ethics and aesthetics. No one can deny that speaking and writing, and communicating with other people in a language, are actions and forms of social behaviour like any others. No one can deny that I make up my mind to say and write such-and-such things for one practical reason or another, and that I must accept responsibility for doing it. I am responsible both for communicating this piece of information to you at this particular time, and also for putting it into these words. You may disapprove of me for telling you, and you may disapprove of me also for having chosen these words in which to tell you. No one can deny also that the forms of language, and the variety of its grammar, arise from this first need of communicating with other people and of instituting and maintaining co-operation and the forms of social life. But it is also true that at a later stage of development men can use language to think, and particularly to think about action, without any immediate need of communicating with others. The thought terminates in a conclusion, which always could be, but need not be, put into words in speech or writing; and the reasons upon which the conclusion was based could be, but need not be, put into words in speech or writing. The step of finding the right words for communication to a possible or actual audience may sometimes be something additional to the drawing of the conclusion and to the recognition of the reasons for it. My thought may have been directed towards a particular person and a particular thing, without my having referred to that person or thing, in the only natural sense of 'refer'; to refer is to make public use of a word or phrase in speech or writing. I may hesitate, and encounter difficulty, in finding the appropriate words to indicate to a particular audience who I am thinking about. This is only one of the many difficulties that I may experience in communicating my thought adequately. It is usually true that if I fail, or find a difficulty, in communicating my thought clearly and accurately, my thought itself is confused. But it is not necessarily and invariably true. The failure or the difficulty may be due to the fact that I have reasons for *saying* something in a certain

way which are different from my reasons for *thinking* that
what I have to say is correct. It is a necessary truth that
there is always at least one clear form of words that will
express the conclusion that I reached in my thought, when
I have reached a clear conclusion about an issue of truth
and falsity. It is a necessary truth also under these conditions that at least one such form of words should be present
to my mind. But I may have difficulty in making clear to
another why I must use just this form of words and no
other; this would be a difficulty only in communication,
and not in my own thought.

The grammatical forms of our language imperfectly
mark the principal differences between types of communication, as expressions of statements, commands, wishes,
promises, undertakings, questions and many others. A
command, a promise, an undertaking exist only in their
expression and as acts of communication, and the question
'Why?' when asked of them, is an inquiry into the reasons
or justification for giving this command, this promise, this
undertaking. These utterances are essentially forms of social
behaviour, the invocation of a social convention, and they
are always liable to be criticised as such. They are criticised
as being in various ways invalid and impermissible, as being
issued in circumstances that are excluded by the conventions governing their correct utterance. At the other extreme, a wish clearly has an existence independent of its
expression, and the question 'Why?' might be either 'Why
do you wish so-and-so?' or 'Why do you express that wish
(here, now)?' Clearly these are widely different questions
and quite different kinds of reason may be invoked in
answer. 'Statement' and 'question' are words that in this
respect stand in an intermediate position between 'wish'
and 'command'. A question that I have not yet put to you

is rather like a wish that I have not yet expressed; but not wholly alike, since the expression of the wish is less essential to its existence as a wish than is the expression of a question to the existence of the question as a question. I may put a certain question to myself and revolve a certain question in my mind. If this is not a purely practical question, but a clear question of truth and falsity, it will already have its appropriate form in words, words that may or may not be spoken aloud. But a wish that I have long entertained may need to be translated into the appropriate words. The wish itself may be comparatively clear and not confused in my mind, but the appropriate expression of it might not be immediately obvious to me. The wish may have existed to some degree outside any social convention, including the convention of language, when a wish approximates to a daydream, the most private and unsocial, and therefore the most personally revealing, of all forms of experience. I may even wish for something that is absurd, in the sense that it could not possibly be realised by any actuality identifiable within our conventions.

There are certainly variations at this point in the vocabularies of different languages; but in general there is an overriding distinction between a belief that I hold, or an item of knowledge that I possess, and the statement that is the expression of this belief or knowledge. We cannot avoid distinguishing between the reasons for which a certain type of statement is commonly made and the grounds upon which a certain type of belief is commonly held. If therefore we look for the function of certain types of statement, as they occur in acts of communication, we do not necessarily arrive at a true account of the logic of our beliefs. It may be true that I ordinarily say 'That is wrong' with a view to persuading somebody not to do something, while I ordinarily say 'That is a bomb' with a view to informing him of what is to be found in front of him. But this fact does not necessarily tell me anything about why I believe, or how I know, that something is wrong, when I do believe or know this, or why I believe, or how I know, that something is a bomb, when I do believe or know this. I may *say* 'That is a beautiful poem' as an expression of admiration or of pleasure, or because I am a critic and a verdict is required of me. But these reasons for saying still leave open the question of my reasons for thinking that it is a beautiful poem. There must be a certain constancy or relatedness in my reasons for thinking that quite different actions were right or quite different things beautiful, if these are to be counted as beliefs at all. To explain this constancy and relatedness in my reasons for thinking is to explain my own moral and aesthetic outlook,or at least some large part of it. A study of the various reasons for which I may communicate my opinions to others is, for the purposes of ethics and aesthetics, secondary. It is true that, if human beings had no means of communicating their opinions and their knowledge to each other, they would not have the means of forming opinions, or of making up their own minds silently and in solitude. The possibility of having beliefs depends upon the possibility of expressing them in statements. This dependence is not a mere contingent matter of fact, a causal dependence in the common order of nature. It is intrinsic to the concept of belief. No sense could be given to a question about the beliefs of beings who possess no language in which to express them, not merely because we could not ascertain their beliefs, but rather because we would not know what would be meant by attributing any specific opinions to them. A belief is essentially something that the believer is ready to express in a statement, even if, for various contingent reasons, he is prevented from expressing it. From this it does not follow that every difference in the syntax and vocabulary of any statement, honestly made, reflects a difference in what is believed by the speaker. Some differences reflect only differences of motive, circumstance and convention surrounding the social act of expressing the belief, and not differences in what the speaker believes. My opinion on a moral or prudential question, whether it is a general and abstract question or a particular case, may be expressed in many different forms: in quasi-imperative form as advice, in a declarative form as a verdict, or in a simple announcement of my decision on the right course of action to be adopted. If moral philosophers concentrate attention upon one or other of these modes of expression, varying, as they do, with social convention and the circumstances of speech, they may neglect the common grounds of belief that lie beneath them. They may conclude that morality is essentially, and at all stages of human development, concerned with recommending or advising, on the grounds that moral judgments (that is, *expressions* of a moral opinion) are often intended as a recommendation or as advice: or that moral opinions are really decisions, because I often express my opinions in the form of a decision on a certain course of action as being the best course open. The intention with which I make moral judgments, that is, express my moral opinions, does not always show the grounds of these opinions. The confusion is between that which is the essential first phase in the development of morality and that which is the essential nature of morality in all its phases. There could not have been unexpressed and rationally grounded moral opinions, unless there had also been the more primitive social acts of giving orders, advice, recommendations, and promulgating rules of conduct. But moral reflection has gone beyond these social acts in the adult men of modern societies. The 'reduction' of moral judgments to quasi-orders and recommendations is like the behaviourist's reduction of inner thoughts and feelings to their natural expression in behaviour: it is a confusion between a necessary pre-condition and the essential nature of that which develops from it.

The ultimate grounds of my opinions will only be made clear to me if I ask myself the question: 'What other changes in my opinions would lead to my changing my opinions on this matter?' Then I clarify my own mind about what it is that I believe and why I believe it. Certainly I can put this question in the form: 'What would lead me to withdraw this statement or to dismiss it as untrue, or as in some other way incorrect?' Wherever I am inquiring into the conditions of application of some concept, this would be the natural way of putting the question, except that the reference to me, as an individual, would be omitted; for I would be concerned with the standard conditions of application of the concept in question, and not with my own dispositions. If I am not inquiring into the conditions of correct, and therefore of intelligible, speech, and into the proper boundaries of a concept that I use in my thought, there is no advantage in expressing the question about the connections of my beliefs in an impersonal form. On the contrary there is a disadvantage, if the impersonal form suggests that ascertaining the order of mutual dependence of my moral beliefs, and their connection with my other opinions, is the same as finding 'the logic' of my assertions. To find 'the logic' of a certain class of assertions is to find the rules of language that determine how particular expressions of the language can be combined intelligibly. I *must* observe these rules if my beliefs are to have substance at all. If I find, when I come to express an opinion, that I cannot express myself within these rules, I thereby find that my belief was confused, a mere muddle. It is logically impossible that there should be a belief, held by someone, that has no natural and correct expression in any language known to the believer. A believer may make several different kinds of mistake in stating his belief; but, if he is to be credited with holding some definite opinion, he must at least be able to recognise a correct expression of his opinion when it is offered to him. The idea of a solitary thinker, who has never used his language in communication with others, cannot be carried through consistently. The expression of a belief is not the inessential act of clothing it with words; it is the only way of making the belief definite, as a belief in this statement rather than that. One cannot consistently conceive of a man asking himself questions about his own beliefs, if he has never literally had any questions put to him. When I reflectively inquire into the connection between my various beliefs, and ask myself whether a change of opinion on one topic would lead me to change my opinion about another, I am confronted with decisions as well as with necessities. I have to sharpen my beliefs and to establish the pattern of rationality to which I commit myself. All this I can do solitarily only because I have learnt to do it in conversation with others. In the domain of opinion, rationality is simply the opposite of disconnectedness, the opposite of holding my opinions apart without forcing myself to range them in a decided order of dependence. Argument with others is the primitive and natural way of finding a decision; fully rational and reflective men learn to do it by themselves, silently.

The relation of an intention to do something and the statement of this intention in words is parallel to the relation of a belief—for example, a belief about the things around me—to its expression in an ordinary declarative statement. So close is the parallel that an intention may be represented as a belief or as knowledge that I am going to do something. To say that I did something intentionally is to say that I knew what I was doing when I did it. So the question that is sometimes asked in amazement and anger: 'Do you know (or realise) what you are saying?' comes to the same as 'Are you saying what you are saying intentionally, or is it an accident, a mistake, unintentional?' In the act of speech, as in any other action, I may not always realise what I am doing, and I may mistake the true nature and immediate effects of my action in making this statement. Alternatively it might be that I was saying something other than I had intended to say, since I was not aware at the time of the necessary implications of my statement. Not realising that I was disclosing a secret would be an example of the first kind of unintentionality; not realising that I have committed myself, by the rules governing the use of the words that I employed, to an opinion that I do not hold is the second kind of unintentionality. 'Did you mean to disclose the secret?' (i.e. 'Did you know that you were disclosing the secret?') is the first kind of inquiry. 'Did you mean so-and-so?', where an implication of the words used is quoted, is the second kind of question. If I answer 'Yes' to the first question, I can be asked for my reason for disclosing the secret. If I answer 'Yes' to the second question, I can be asked for my reason for believing that the implied statement is true. The similarity and the difference between these two questions about reasons is, and always has been, a large part of the subject-matter of moral philosophy.

How close is the analogy between a good and sufficient reason for doing something and a good and sufficient reason for believing something?

It seems that the range of facts that *could* (logically) be given as reasons for believing something is limited by the content of the statement believed. It may seem that the range of facts that could be quoted, without contradiction or logical absurdity, as reasons for doing something is limited only by the interests and desires of the speaker. This difference, or some variant of it, may seem to lie in the nature of intentional action as opposed to intentional thought. Nothing will count as 'thought', and therefore as 'belief', without a certain minimum of statable consistency and rule in the transition from ground to conclusion. It may seem that a person's action is independently identifiable as an event in the world, and that, however inconsistent and irregular a man may be in the reasons that lead him to act, the actions are still identifiable as actions of his, however irrational they may be.

This contrast is at least questionable. A certain minimum of consistency and regularity is required in behaviour, if that behaviour is to be counted as intentional human action at all. There is here also the requirement of connectedness, of a trajectory of intention that fits a sequence of behaviour into an intelligible whole, intelligible as having a direction, the direction of means towards an end. The external view of a particular action, as a change in the world caused by a particular person's movement, is not enough to identify the action as a case of a person's doing so-and-so, unless the intention is known or inferred. As soon as the intention guiding the movement is stated, only a limited range of reasons could intelligibly be quoted as reasons for doing the action in question. Just as some putative reasons for believing that so-and-so is true would seem so irregular and unconnected with the conclusion as not to count as reasons at all, so some putative reasons for doing so-and-so would seem so unconnected with the action as not to count as reasons at all. It is not true that absolutely *any* thought, impulse or sentiment could equally well be mentioned by me in giving my reasons for behaving in a certain specific way. In specifying what I was doing, I have already indicated that which I was trying to achieve, and I could not have wanted to achieve something that was entirely at variance with that which I actually intended to achieve. I cannot be said genuinely to want anything (x) unless I take the fact that something (y) is a means toward x as a reason for doing y. But it would be wrong to infer, following Aristotle, that whatever I deliberately do must be directed towards some end that I want, which would imply that any statement of my reason for acting can begin with the words 'I wanted.' 'I did not want to do this, but I thought that it would be wrong not to do it' does not need completion by the idea of an ulterior desire to do the right thing. But I cannot (logically) too constantly act against my alleged desires and still maintain that I genuinely want that which I never pursue in action when the opportunity is given to me. Some minimal consistency in the relation between statements of wants and ambitions and actual habits of performance is essential to the idea of intentional action.

To review the reason, or reasons, for an action is sometimes to review a train of thought, or a calculation, leading up to a conclusion, as the reason or reasons for a belief constitute a train of thought, or a calculation, leading up to a conclusion. But a sentiment and mood are obviously more common, more naturally intelligible and less disreputable as the given reason, and even as the justification, for my having acted in a certain way than they would be as the reason for my having believed something. They could sometimes be the reason why, as a matter of fact, I believed what I was told; they could not be the justification of the belief. It is a necessary truth that part of the point and purpose of any belief, no matter on what topic, is to be calculated. 'I simply believed it on an impulse' is an admission of a lapse, a failure, an absurdity. 'I simply did it on an impulse' is not necessarily, and for everyone, an admission of a lapse, failure, or absurdity. It is not equally obvious that it is the point or purpose of any action, no matter what kind of action, to be calculated. But a greater difference lies in the nature of the conclusion: principally, that I may be unable to form, or may refrain from forming, any conclusion in a matter of belief, while I am in the end unavoidably driven to some conclusion in a practical matter, if this is a question of what I am myself to do in a situation confronting me. In an immediate practical issue, there is nothing that corresponds to suspending judgment and to having no opinion on a question proposed. Even if I cannot decide *that* one of the only two courses open to me is right and that the other is wrong, I must decide *to* do either one or the other.

Any one person must exhibit, in any short period of his life, a certain degree of consistency in the passage from reason to belief and from reason to action. The reasons that he gives for his beliefs, and the reasons that he gives for his actions, must equally fit together over some period of time into a recognisable policy of belief, or policy of action, in order to count as genuine reasons. The word 'policy', naturally applied to action rather than to belief, shows this necessity. If I have disclosed some information to someone, and I am asked why I did this, I am being asked for the policy of which my action was a part, a policy that was not immediately obvious to the questioner. Should I answer: 'There was no particular reason: I just did it', I would in effect be repudiating the suggestion that my action was part of some larger policy. If I supply a reason for the action, I fit it into the policy of which it was part. It is plain then that this explanation of this action must not be wholly inconsistent with the explanations offered for other actions during the same period of time. The explanations must show me as following one or more policies at that time, each of which can also be regarded as larger actions. The idea of a rational action requires the doing of something within the penumbra of a larger intention, as the idea of a rational belief requires an acceptance of some statement within an environment of other statements accepted. There is in this respect no *absolute* difference between the question 'Why do you say that?' where this is intended as an inquiry into the grounds of the assertion, and 'Why do you say that?' where this is an inquiry into the reasons for making this particular assertion on this particular occasion. The real difference here is that the action necessarily has a date and necessarily was performed at a particular time and in a particular place. The consisttency of intention that is necessary to rational, as opposed to impulsive or unreflective, action is the consistency of a policy that wholly occupies a particular period of time, however short. It follows that the relation of the reason to the action cannot be criticised in some of the ways, and by some of the standards, that are appropriate to the criticism of beliefs. It is not unintelligible that the same man should have been impelled to act for different reasons, or even different kinds of reason, at widely separated times. On one occasion he was following one policy, on another a different, and perhaps an opposing policy. Some of his beliefs may also be supported by quite different arguments, or kinds of argument, at different periods in his life. But beliefs generally (there are exceptions) must be to some degree stable if they are to count as beliefs at all. They are not in their nature episodic, as are actions with their accompanying intentions. Any one man inevitably carries with him an enormous load of settled beliefs about the world, which he never has had occasion to question and many of which he never has had occasion to state. They constitute the generally unchanging background of his active thought and observation, and they constitute also his knowledge of his own position in the world in relation to other things. The culture of which he is part is formed partly by the beliefs in which he grew up, almost without noticing them, and partly by the habits of action and social behaviour that are unthinking, unquestioned, but not unintentional.

Still the difference between reasons for belief and reasons for action, in the requirement of consistency, has been understated. The whole point and purpose of a belief, and of the kind of thought that leads up to it, is that it should be true, true whoever states it and on whatever occasion it is stated in the form appropriate to that occasion. Truth presupposes conventions of interpretation. One does not in general need to consider the occasion on which a belief was formed in somebody's mind in order to decide upon its truth, in the same way that one generally needs to consider the occasion upon which an action was performed in order to decide upon its rightness. The content of the belief, fixed by the conventions of language, determines by itself the reasons that are required to support it, independently of any temporary occasion of its assertion. An action does not have a content, even if it is the act of saying something or of performing some ritual; it only invites a description and an interpretation, the description of what was actually done and an account of the intention with which it was done. Therefore there is no means of establishing a *universal* connection between a specified action, and the reasons for and against performing it, in virtue of which certain reasons *must* be accepted as good reasons independently of everything else. The only *universal necessity* is that any one man at any one time should be sufficiently regular and consistent in his reasons for doing whatever he is doing for his conduct to count as intentional. Any answer to the question 'Why did you say that?', interpreted as asking for the grounds of the opinion expressed, is exposed to the objection that the grounds given are under any conditions, and for anyone, unacceptable or insufficient grounds for the opinion; and this unacceptableness and insufficiency can be demonstrated universally and solely by reference to the content of the belief expressed. Any answer to the question 'Why did you disclose that information?' necessarily mentions the particular occasion of this particular act, and it is not *necessarily* true that reasons that are bad reasons for acting in this way on this occasion would always be bad reasons for acting in that way. 'If that is your reason, I no longer understand what it is that you believe: you must be using words in a different sense'—this would be the natural answer to some reasons given, if they are wholly irrelevant to the content of the belief professed. The corresponding incomprehension of reasons given for an action would be: 'If that was your reason, I wholly misunderstood your intention; I misinterpreted what you were trying to do.'

The intention of a deliberate action has to be grasped by the spectator, who sees it as aimed at a certain result and perhaps as the putting into effect of a certain principle. But the perceived phenomenon of the agent in action, regarded as a set of movements and perceptible changes, is not correlated with the intention behind it by rules and conventions, as words are correlated with their meanings by rules and conventions. An observer cannot distinguish the subjective intention from the actual meaning of the action, as he can sometimes distinguish the meaning that a speaker has intended his words to convey from their true meaning according to the rules of the language. There is no such thing as the 'standard meaning' of an action, unless it is itself a symbolic or ritual performance. There is only the intended effect or achievement and the actual effect or achievement. When these two fall apart, the mistake that has been made is not due to ignorance or neglect of a human convention, and no reference to human convention is involved in showing that the actual achievement was not the intended one. The 'inside' of an action, its sense or meaning, is wholly in the thought and purpose of the agent, which cannot properly be said to be expressed in action in the same sense in which his beliefs are expressed in words. To express his belief in words he must find within a language the right words to represent his thought *correctly*, the thought taking shape in these words, even though it might have been expressed in another language and in other words. Putting a plan or principle into effect in action does not leave a choice of alternative systems of expression and of finding the conventionally correct expression within these systems. This could only be said of an action regarded as having a conventional meaning in the same sense that the words of a language have a conventional meaning. I might, for example, have to choose between nodding my head and holding up my hand as two ways of expressing my agreement. Nodding my head in this social situation is saying something. Actions do not always, or even generally, have a meaning, in this sense of a conventional meaning. But they always have a sense or direction that is bestowed upon them by the particular agent at that particular time, if they are intentional.

Admittedly an artificial restriction is being imposed upon the indeterminate notion of an action. When I make a gesture, when I speak, or write, or communicate in some other way, I have performed an action which is distinguished, and characterised, by the conventional meaning of the symbolic actions that I perform. We do try, in ordinary speech and thought, to keep the distinction between thought and action as definite as possible. To think, to draw conclusions and to speculate, is not thought of as a form of action, but rather as the introduction to action. But to communicate my thoughts to another is always to act, because it makes some change in the world. That which I do is that for which I am responsible and which is peculiarly an expression of myself. It is essential to thought that it takes its own forms and follows its own paths without my intervention, that is, without the intervention of my will. I identify myself with my will. Thought, when it is most pure, is self-directing, as in the exercise of the intellect in deduction and in the following of an argument. When I use the active verbs of will and speak of directing my thoughts to a certain topic, or of concentrating my attention on it, I still contrast these acts of will, which start the process, from the process itself. Thought begins on its own path, governed by its universal

153

rules, when the preliminary work of the will is done. No process of thought could be punctuated by acts of will, voluntary switchings of attention, and retain its status as a continuous process of thought.

It may still be said that each man has his own style and distinguishing manner of thought, the topics to which his mind naturally returns and the order in which he approaches them in this thought. This is undeniable fact. These are marks of personality which, like mannerisms in behaviour, he may himself seek to control. The natural and characteristic movement of my thoughts becomes known, both to myself and to others, as a recognisable feature of mine, only through the expression of my thought. I can be distinguished from every other thing in the world as the man who said so-and-so at such-and-such an exactly marked time and place; it would seem unnatural to count my thinking about so-and-so as an action, even if it is a possible answer to the question 'What were you doing there at that time?'—'I was thinking about so-and-so'. It would be unnatural, because my thinking about so-and-so would not ordinarily be thought of as the bringing about of some recognisable change in the world; and this seems essential to the idea of action. To list the essential features of an action already noticed: (*a*) that it is something done at will and (*b*) at some particular time, (*c*) that it constitutes some recognisable change in the world. The words used here are certainly too vague and unclear to constitute any kind of analysis of the indeterminate idea of action. What could be the test of whether a verb stands for something that is 'a bringing about of a recognisable change in the world'? But these vaguely expressed ideas do go together to form the commonplace notion of action, which is ordinarily contrasted with the 'inner' processes of thought and feeling, which are preliminary to action. One must first follow these ideas and test their validity, if the range and nature of morality, as it is now understood, is to be made clear. The contrast between 'inner' and 'external' processes is closely connected with the contrast between that which is a source of action, or the effect of action, and that which is the bringing about of a change in the world. For this reason among others, it has seemed wrong to represent a belief that a certain statement is true, the assent that is the conclusion of a train of thought, as an action, even though one can speak of withholding assent or suspending disbelief. There is a whole range of idioms that assimilate belief to action—e.g. 'I cannot believe', or even 'I cannot bring myself to believe', or 'You ought not to believe', or 'He refused to believe'. We may blame people for believing something too readily or for not suspending judgment. On the other hand it may seem exaggerated to speak of someone as responsible for his own beliefs. It would seem logically absurd to prohibit by law the holding of certain beliefs, if having the beliefs was distinguished from expressing them. This logical absurdity was remarked by Spinoza, opposing Descartes' picture of assent to a proposition as an act of will, which each man is free to control as he chooses. This point of difference in the philosophy of mind between Descartes and Spinoza is of the greatest importance in the assessment of human powers and virtues: indeed it is one of the dividing lines of philosophy.

The difficulty is to see by what method of argument the difference could possibly be settled. Exactly at these dividing lines, when a decision has to be made between two conceptions of personality, the method of examining established concepts, as they occur in contemporary speech, is inadequate. There is no way of showing that the idioms in common speech which point to one decision are to be preferred to the idioms which point to an opposite decision. Even were there such a method of decision by reference to current linguistic usage, one could still ask oneself whether accepted contemporary usage is not tied to a disputable moral outlook: tied, in the sense that the domain of responsible action, of actions done at will and making some change in the external world, is marked off as that domain of total human activity and expression which is considered most important and valuable, the most in need of encouragement or prohibition. It may be that in a society in which a man's theoretical opinions and religious beliefs were held to be supremely important, a man's beliefs would be considered as much part of his responsibility as his behaviour to other men. In a culture that is largely utilitarian in its outlook, a sharper distinction might be made between inner life and responsible action. We cannot assume that the formation of concepts of personality and the formation of a moral outlook have in fact been held apart, or even that they can ever be held apart. A particular moral outlook, connected with particular forms of social life, will show itself in the distinctions that are stressed in the forms of common speech. The only honest method would be to review the various recognised concepts of action, together with their moral and evaluative implications, and to look for more general moral grounds for making some choice between them.

If assenting to a proposition in one's mind, or accepting some conclusion in one's mind, is regarded as an action, the force of the word 'action' here might be that one is free to believe or not to believe, in the same sense that one is free either to leave the room or to remain sitting in the chair.

But it is a necessary feature of anything that can be called an action that one might on occasion want to do it and also decide to do it and yet for some reason fail to achieve the result. This double face of human action, the one face being the project and the other the result, is essential and ineliminable. If I act, there must be both the intention to make a change, and the change intended, but possibly not achieved. It is generally the achievement, actual or unsuccessfully aimed at, that gives a name and recognisable character to my activities, not only to others but also to myself. It follows that, given any identifiable action, there must generally be the logical possibility of intending but not succeeding, the antithesis of attempt and success. There must therefore be a method of distinguishing an attempt that falls short from an attempt that succeeds for each distinguishable class of action, even if the method can sometimes be applied only by the agent himself; he at least must be in a position to know that he has, or has not, achieved what he intends. In the case of belief, it is not clear what counts as trying and intending to believe something, but failing in the attempt, although these phrases are sometimes used. I may well say in ordinary conversation 'I want to believe what you are telling me, but I cannot'. But the statement of a difficulty in the 'attempt' is already a statement that I do not believe and is not seriously meant. If I was told that I could satisfy my desire to believe by turning my attention away from the contrary evidence, I would not call my ensuing state, brought into existence by these means, belief. It seems that I cannot present my own belief in something as an achievement, because, by so presenting it, I would disqualify it as belief. 'I have finally made myself believe him', or 'I am determined to believe whatever he tells me', are virtually professions of scepticism. I could represent an *announcement*, or *confession*, of belief, as an achievement, as something that I might try and, under certain circumstances, fail to make. Similarly, I could represent the learning of something, or the acquiring of information, as something that I might attempt and fail to achieve. But when a statement is brought to my attention, and the question is whether I believe it or not, the decision that I announce in the words 'Yes, I believe it' is not a decision to do anything; nor can these words constitute an announcement that I have attempted or achieved anything. I have not decided *to* believe; I have decided *that* the statement in question is true. This deciding, which is a deciding *that*, is not naturally represented as an action, since there is no sense in which I could intend, or decide, to decide that a statement is true. One might intelligibly speak of oneself as discovering, or realising, that one had for some time believed a certain story to be true, without having explicitly acknowledged to oneself that one did believe it. The acknowledgment is then acknowledgment of an existing state of mind.

We make a contrast between our intentions and beliefs, together constituting thought, and the actions and judgments that flow from them, since thought is at once the background and the source both of action and of statement. Thought is necessarily directed outwards towards action or judgment or both. If I say that I am thinking, or if I say that I am thinking about so-and-so, I am understood to imply that I am trying to arrive at some conclusion either about a possible action or about a possible judgment. 'I am thinking' invites the question 'What is the question?' or 'What is the problem?' and it is logically necessary that there should be some answer to this question, and an answer that points to some possible action, or to some possible judgment before me, to be either accepted or rejected. Thought cannot be thought, as opposed to daydreaming or musing, unless it is directed towards a conclusion, whether in action or in judgment. Intentions that were never put into practice would not count as genuine intentions, and beliefs which were never honestly expressed and which never guided action, would not count as beliefs. A man who with apparent sincerity professed intentions, which were never in fact translated into action, would finally be held not seriously or 'really' to intend that which he declared that he intended to do, even if there was no suggestion of deceit. He would be compelled, by mere respect for the meaning of words, to admit to himself that his so-called intentions were more properly described as vague velleities or idle hopes. A man who with apparent sincerity professed beliefs upon which he never acted, supposing the beliefs to be of a kind relevant to action, or who claimed beliefs from which he never drew the regular conclusions, would be said to be holding these beliefs in words only, but not truly believing. If a man is to attach any meaning to the alternative of belief or disbelief, he must in each case envisage some possible consequence, upon his own actions or expectations or possible future utterances, of his coming down on one side or the other in his own mind. The idea of thought as an interior monologue, and of beliefs forming themselves in the mind without being expressed, will become altogether empty, if the thought does not even purport to be directed towards its issue in the external world on some conceivable occasion. Under these conditions thought and belief would not differ from the charmed and habitual rehearsal of phrases, or the drifting of ideas through the mind.

The act of assent to a statement, saying 'Yes', is a

genuine act, recognisable and carrying its own consequences with it, when it is a public affirmation, an answer
to a question actually asked. We may comment on the
manner in which the act was performed, whether it was
hesitant, aggressive, or shy. The assent, that takes place
within the mind and in no process of communication,
when no question has been actually asked and answered,
is a shadowy assent and a shadowy act. One would be
speaking metaphorically if one described the manner of the
performance, since, strictly speaking, there was no performance. If I came firmly or hesitantly to a certain conclusion in my own mind, the firmness or hesitancy refer to
the appropriate expression of the argument and of the
conclusion. The dramatic story that someone may honestly
tell of his doubts, waverings, self-questioning and final
assent is a kind of disclosure that we can understand and
accept. This is the story of how his thought *would* have
been expressed, at the appropriate times, if it had been
expressed at all. But we would reject such an account of
the thought of another, suggested to us by a third person,
if the thinker referred to never expressed himself, and was
never likely to express himself, in the terms now used to
describe his mental struggle. His silent thought must be
the shadow of the expression that is natural to him, as an
individual.

This metaphor of 'shadow' is almost unavoidable,
because it is peculiarly appropriate. We do think of the
activities of the thinking mind as the shadows cast by
publicly perceptible statements and actions. The play of
the mind, free of any expression in audible speech or
visible action, is a reality, as the play of shadows is a reality.
But any description of it is derived from the description of
its natural expression in speech and action, as a description

of the play of shadows is a description of the movement of some corresponding bodies, which are not necessarily the bodies that cast the shadows. If we had not encountered and classified the movement of bodies in the way that we have, we would not interpret and describe the play of shadows in the way that we do. If we did not ask questions in speech, we would not recognise the occasions on which we can be said to be asking ourselves questions in our own thought. We do really hesitate and encounter difficulties in our thought, in the same sense that shadows on the window-pane do really move and come in contact with other shadows. It is not a strained metaphor that I use when I speak of the shadow's movement, and it is no more a strained metaphor to speak of the questions that I put to myself. Yet we think of the movement of the shadow on the window-pane as less substantial, as more dependent for its existence on someone's perception and recognition of it, than the movement of a body. For the same reasons, we think of the question that I silently ask myself as a less substantial episode, as an episode more dependent for its existence on my recognition of it, than the question that I put to another in conversation. 'Did you ask yourself this question at the time?' is an inquiry into an event that is less definitely marked as having occurred or not occurred than the event referred to in the inquiry 'Did you ask him this question at that time?' The indefiniteness of a mental event of this kind is like the indefiniteness of a shadow in comparison with the hard outlines of a body defined by physical contact. Statements about the outlines of a physical object are definitely testable, because their truth can be ascertained and confirmed by several different kinds of observation made by different persons and by the use of different senses. One can speak therefore of a procedure of confirming that the outlines are in fact what they seemed at first sight to be. The indefiniteness of statements about the shadow's outline is the absence of a procedure of confirming, from different points of view and by the use of different senses, that they are in fact what they seem to be at first sight. This last contrast between appearance and reality almost loses its sense here. The indefiniteness comes out in the many occasions when it would not be possible to give a true and unqualified answer—'Yes, it happened' or 'No, it did not'. We have to interpret the processes of our own thought and reflection rather than simply to record them, as we may simply record the course of a conversation, with a definite and variously ascertainable accuracy or inaccuracy.

It may be objected that the mere acts of speaking and of writing, of making a noise and making marks on paper, cannot be said to be the substantial reality of human thought, of which silent reflection is the insubstantial shadow. A man might mutter to himself, just audibly, when he is thinking, or mutter to himself just inaudibly. Why will this audibility make the processes of his thought definite? The answer is that the definiteness depends on the possibility of the process of thought being recognised, scrutinised and identified by observers from different points of view; this possibility is essential to any definite reality. The process of thought that may occupy a man's mind, when he is in fact talking of something quite different, is, as an occurrence, indefinite, because there is no possibility of anyone, including the man himself, later scrutinising it to make sure that it in fact followed a certain course, once a doubt has been raised. His spoken thought might have been heard by several people, who could check their memories and observations against each other. It emerged into the world of things that can be observed from many points of view, the only substantial and solid world that there is, or that there could be. Although this is a distinction that admits of degree, an act of speech or of writing gives my thought a body and substance, makes it a solid object for assessment. There is the possibility of looking again at the writing to see that my thought really was what I seem to remember that it was, or of asking witnesses that I did say what I seem to myself to remember that I said. My unspoken beliefs and questionings remain always, to a greater or less degree, shadowy and uncertain even to myself. I have to go into action of some kind, even if it is only the minimal action of muttering to myself, if I or anyone else is to be sure what I do definitely think. I have to embody my thought, which is in this sense parasitic upon its expression. The question of whether I did or did not agree with, or accept in my own mind, that which you said to me at that moment has a logical indefiniteness that distinguishes it from the question of whether I actually said 'Yes' or 'No'. The question of unexpressed agreement could never even have arisen if there had not been the possibility of my saying 'Yes' or 'No'. My unexpressed agreement simply consisted in my disposition to say 'Yes', which was for some reason inhibited.

This principle of the parasitic and shadowy nature of mental actions is of some consequence. It implies that anything that I can be said to do is primarily identifiable as a change that I recognisably make in the common world of things, and that, corresponding to any such primarily identifiable action, there may be an arrested or inhibited form of it, when the publicly identifiable change is not actually made. As my intention to act in a certain way is related to the overt action intended, so my belief at a particular moment that a statement is true is related to an affirmation of it. This relation can be rendered by representing the truncated or arrested action, the momentary intention or belief, as a *disposition* to act, or publicly to affirm, in a certain way. Unfortunately the word 'disposition' has been used in too many different senses. The shadow-relation of mental act to full or genuine act can be better indicated by an analogy. Suppose a man is insulted: it may be said of him, metaphorically, that he 'looked daggers' at his attacker, or that 'if looks could kill', his look would have done so. His expression was that of a man killing or striking, but he did not kill or strike. The real action was arrested, and we saw only the shadow of it. One can suppose now that not only is the action inhibited, but the facial expression also; the man deliberately controls his face. Then the remainder is the mental content, the attitude or state of mind that constitutes the man's reaction to the insult. Similarly, having heard something said, I hold my tongue and I do not say 'No', as I am inclined to: what remains is my disbelief in what is said. If I had never had the power of saying 'No', and if I did not have the power of inhibiting my actions, it would never be right to attribute unexpressed beliefs to me. A man to whom we attribute a rich inner life of belief and disbelief, of unexpressed doubt and self-questioning, must be a man of great powers of self-restraint, to whom the inhibition of action is natural. He has cut away the substance of human routines and chosen to live with their shadow. He does not shout but he exults inwardly; he does not weep, but he feels sad. He does not ask questions, but he doubts; he does not deny, but he disbelieves. This habit of inhibition, which replaces the substance of perceptible behaviour with its shadow in the mental life of thought and feeling, is the process of civilisation. Manners create the inner life of the mind by placing barriers in front of the immediate and natural expressions of thought and feeling. The mental and inner life of men is the obverse of social restraint and convention.

If the word 'disposition' is used in the sense of a 'set', or of the predisposition to act which remains when overt action is inhibited, it is appropriate to the analysis of mental concepts. This is the sense of 'disposed to' in which 'disposed to' could be substituted for 'wanted to' in the sentences—'I wanted to sneeze, but I managed to stop myself', or 'I wanted to laugh but I restrained myself'. Whenever a distinct verb has been introduced for the inhibited state, and the corresponding action is normally a voluntary action, this verb will naturally be said to represent a mental act. We have in fact a sophisticated vocabulary of shadow actions, with various processes in silent thought made parallel to their corresponding phrases in argument and conversation. But often the same verbs—for example 'infer' and 'think' are used indifferently for the truncated action or process and its completed, overt form. Those philosophers fall into absurdity who suppose that the public actions of making meaningful statements and of asking questions must be said to be *accompanied* by a corresponding shadow process. The shadow is that which remains when the public aspect of the action is inhibited; therefore it does not need to be added to the whole of which it is a detachable part. In general there is an inner process of thought and reflection whenever outward-going action is for some reason blocked or arrested. When I am fully engaged in some intelligent activity, including the activities of writing and talking, I cannot easily single out from within the whole activity a purely mental compo-

nent, except by deliberately arresting my physical movements and utterances. That which remains during the
pause for reflection would no longer naturally be called the
mental component of the activity. It becomes autonomous
and self-contained in its own indefinite way. But when I
have a settled intention to act in a certain way in the
future, this intelligent and thoughtful disposition is, while
it lasts, separated from the action that will later incor
porate it.

If this account of the relation of thought to action is
correct, it follows that my reasons for acting, including the
making of a statement among actions, are on a different
level from my reasons for believing a statement to be true.
To state my reasons for believing something is to state
what I would want to say in an argument arising from a
denial of the original statement. I am here wholly concerned with what I would want to *say*, with the sequence of
statements that I would want to make, with 'ands' and
'therefores' inserted between them. But in giving my
reasons for behaving in a certain way, I am making a connection between what I think, in the sense of what I am
disposed to assert, and that which I am doing, that is, with
some change that I am trying to achieve. In philosophy
one ought surely to find this last connection altogether
mysterious. In meeting this mystery Aristotle introduced
the concept of wanting. He thought that any answer to the
question 'Why are you doing that?' *must* be of the form 'I
want so-and-so and I calculate that so-and-so'. No other
form of answer would be intelligible as an explanation of
action. Any answer of the form 'I am doing this because I
believe so-and-so' would be unintelligible, unless it was
understood to be elliptical, with the 'and I want' clause
implicit. Aristotle curtly put this principle of explanation

in the slogan: 'Reason by itself does not move (sc. to action)'. Since an action is a movement, a making of a change, the source of motion has to be found in an appetite or wish. The work of thought is to formulate the desire and to identify its object and to discover the proper means to attaining the end desired. Planning entails knowing what one wants, and knowing what one wants entails being able to specify and identify what one wants. The reason for an action has been given when the agent's conception of the end has been explained together with his calculation of the means to it. We then see the fusion of the thinking, which is an inhibited discussion of the end desired and of the means to it, and the mere wanting. The reason for the action is a fusion of these two elements, because the representation to myself in words of an object desired modifies the direction, and sometimes the intensity, of the original, blind appetite. The desires develop and change direction in the process of elaborating in thought the possible ends of conduct, as in a Homeric council of war new courses of action are suggested and acclaimed.

This scheme of deliberate action, and of the form of explanation appropriate to it, can scarcely be appraised as either true or false; for it is not clear what could be the basis of assessment, or what kind of evidence could be decisive. In ordinary speech and in ordinary circumstances we do in fact look for and accept explanations of human conduct that are more or less in accordance with this scheme. But one cannot find a principle that runs through the whole range of those reasons for action which may under different conditions be found acceptable in ordinary speech. Any scheme that is as clear and definite as Aristotle's will exclude some kinds of explanation that are in fact given and accepted, just because the scheme is clear and definite. There is still no compelling ground for insisting that the word 'want' *must* enter into every full statement of reasons for acting. There are too many different levels of rationality and deliberateness in conduct, too many varieties of half-intentional action and half-conscious thought, for any tidy formula to fit. There is no possibility of devising a simple machinery of the mind in terms of which to explain the indefinite varieties of human conduct. We know now, as Aristotle did not, that we still know too little of the workings of the unconscious mind. We see that our own concepts are confused by new discoveries in this domain; we do not yet know how they will be replaced and improved as a new science develops. In philosophy one can indicate the nature and source of the confusion, and the points at which our mental concepts are now beginning to break down in application: and we can show why mental concepts must always differ, in the conditions of their application, from physical concepts. After that any philosopher has to make a choice of a set of explanatory terms which bring out the distinctions, already present in common speech, that he particularly wants to stress. At this point he unavoidably enters the domain of morality. He has to say how human conduct should be viewed and judged; and 'should' here has a moral connotation.

Chapter 3

ACTION AND SELF-CONSCIOUSNESS

A T any moment in any man's waking and conscious life
there is always a set of possible true answers to the
questions—'What is he doing now?' For human beings, to
be conscious is to have active intentions. Within the set of
possible true answers to this question there is a smaller set
of answers which the person himself would give if he was
asked what he was doing. These constitute the set of things
that he knows that he is doing and that are not done
unintentionally. Within this sub-set of things which he
knows that he is doing there is at least one description that
he himself would give, if he wished to be honest, as an
account of the main direction of his attention at this
particular moment. Even when he is wholly absorbed in
something that he himself would call a single activity, and
when his attention is in no way divided, there is necessarily
a variety of true accounts that could in principle be
offered of this single activity. But there is generally one
account that seems to him peculiarly appropriate to his
present intentions, when his intentions are not exceptionally complicated. He may be aware of himself as doing
more than one thing at the time; his active intentions may
be more or less equally divided. Even when his active
intentions and interest are divided, these intentions constitute for him the particular point of his present activity.
He himself is normally accepted as the final authority in
declaring what his central intention is, or what his main
intentions are, at any particular moment. Its centrality is

the fact that he would immediately and naturally mention these projects as occupying his attention if he were asked what he was doing. About a kind of creature that does not have the means to say what it is primarily interested in doing at any particular moment, it would not even make sense to ask what its central intention is. It would fail to make sense, not because the intention could not be *communicated*, but because *having* an intention in the forefront of the mind is necessarily connected with thinking of this activity before others, with having it in mind as the meaning of one's present posture; and thinking is necessarily connected with having the means of expressing thought. Certainly there are conditions in which a man's intentions are deeply confused in his own mind without a lapse into unconsciousness or madness. But they could not be *totally* confused, while he is conscious and sane, because he must at least know what he is trying to do in relation to *some* of the objects identifiable around him. Lastly, his active intentions necessarily entail some certainty in his own mind about the future; at any moment he knows what he is about to do next because he knows what he is trying to do now. He has one or more projects that extend forward in time, even when his behaviour is for some reason abnormally disconnected and spasmodic, like the behaviour of very small children, to whom intentions can scarcely be attributed.

Within the concept of action lies the distinction between an attempt and an achievement. It has been suggested that there is no limit to what a man can try to do; he can try to do anything that he chooses, provided that he has some idea of how it might possibly be done. There is a limit, discoverable in experience, upon what he can achieve, that is, upon what he will actually succeed in doing if he tries. There may be occasions on which he is not in a position, in either a literal or metaphorical sense, to make an attempt to achieve a certain result. We may then say 'He could not even have tried'. Even on such occasions he might have tried to get himself into the required position to make the attempt, and this could be counted as making the attempt, because he is taking the first steps towards the achievement in view. This regress of responsibility can be extended indefinitely, whatever obstructions are supposed. Every obstruction in the line of action is something of which the acting subject could in principle be aware. When he is aware of an obstruction to his intention, he has the choice between attempting, and not attempting, to circumvent it. Reviewing the situation critically and from the outside, and in retrospect, an observer may ask at least three questions about any impediment to a particular action. First, whether the agent was aware of it, secondly, whether he tried to overcome it, and, if the answer is negative, the third question is, whether he would have succeeded if he had tried. The first question does not present itself at all as a question to the agent himself before action. The corresponding question that the agent can put to himself is—'Have I noticed and taken account of all the impediments to my intended action?' The second, 'Shall I try or not?' presents itself to the agent before action as a question for decision, and not for prediction. The third—'Would I succeed if I tried?'—calls for the agent's prediction. Here we have noted one necessary difference between action as attempt and action as achievement. When the question 'Will I hit it or not?' is intended as 'Will I make the attempt to hit it or not?' it must be a preliminary to a decision and it cannot be a call for a prediction. When the question is intended as 'Will I succeed in hitting it or not?' it must be a preliminary to a prediction and it cannot be a call for a decision. If I speak of myself as having decided to succeed next time in some undertaking, as perhaps I might, I am taken to be expressing a mood of determination, or a will to succeed, in a particularly emphatic form, together with some confidence that I will in fact succeed. But I cannot take my decision to succeed as the sole ground of my belief that I will in fact succeed; this would be a belief in magic. I both can and must take my decision to make the attempt as both the necessary and sufficient 'ground' for my certainty that I am in fact going to make the attempt. The word 'ground' is indeed too weak. I cannot distinguish my certainty that I shall make the attempt as something apart from the decision to make it. But it will be asked—What is the force of 'will in fact make the attempt'? There must be an action, or a set of actions, that constitute the attempt, and the occurrence or non-occurrence of these actions determines whether or not the attempt has been made. Each of these actions will have its double face, as something attempted and something achieved. Therefore it may seem that his own prediction that he will not succeed in one of the actions that constitute the attempt would be a. prediction that he will not make the attempt; and this is contrary to the hypothesis that a man cannot predict his own attempts, but can only decide upon them. The false step in this argument is the *identification* of making the attempt with doing the things that on this occasion constitute making the attempt. To decide to try to do something is one decision, and to decide on certain specific actions, considered to be necessary to success, is another decision. When I decide that I shall try to achieve a certain result, I thereby decide to take some appropriate steps, whatever they are. But I do not thereby decide to take certain specific steps. 'I have decided to try to persuade him' does not entail any statement of the form 'I have decided to put the following specific argument to him . . .' Having made the decision to try, I then have to decide what is the best way of achieving the end in view in the particular circumstances of the moment. A prediction that I will not in fact take the steps, or perform any of the actions, that are in fact necessary is not a prediction that I will or will not make the attempt. It would only constitute a prediction that I will or will not succeed in the attempt. Provided that I do *something*, and take some first step, that can be indicated as part of my attempt to achieve the result, the failure of the consequences that should follow this first step is still a failure in the attempt.

But, once again, is it logically impossible that a man should predict, rightly or wrongly, what he himself will try to do in the future? Suppose that a fellow prisoner says to me: 'I predict that you will try to escape before your time is finished', and that I reply 'I am sure that you are right, and I am equally sure that I will fail in the attempt'. Upon what principle is the title of 'prediction' refused to the first part of the reply, and accorded to the second part? The answer given in the previous chapter was that an inductive argument could not properly be the basis of the first statement and that it must be the basis of the second. But why should not a man, as a disinterested observer of himself, reflect upon his own record and take his own record as a basis for predicting his own future actions? 'I expect that I shall try to escape *at some time*' might be intended more as a prediction than as a statement of intention, if the occasion of the escape is left entirely undetermined. The speaker might be admitting that he has a tendency to try to escape sooner or later, as the evidence of his record shows. A man can examine the record of his own performances disinterestedly, and notice regularities in them, as he would examine the record of another. If the action is located in the undetermined and remote future and does not call for any early decision, a quasi-prediction, or half-prediction, is just possible. The notion of logical possibility, as it is generally used now, is not helpful here: for it only takes one back to the more superficial question of whether we should *call* a proposition of a certain type a prediction or whether we should *call* it the announcement of a decision. We need rather to see the situation that imposes these related distinctions upon us: attempt—achievement and decision—prediction.

There are points in our discourse at which we are compelled to think dialectically, that is, to acknowledge the possibility of an objective contradiction, which arises when two lines of thought, each legitimate within their limits, are pressed too far beyond these limits. The contradiction is objective, in the sense that it does not arise merely from carelessness or ignorance in the use of words. The contradiction here arises from the situation of a speaker speaking about himself as he would commonly speak about others, and simultaneously making a double reference to himself; first, as the observer of himself, who is the author of the statement, and, second, as the independent agent observed. I can make a double reference to myself without contradiction, when I refer to myself, first, as the person observing and, secondly, as the person observed. I may become aware of myself as someone who is trying to annoy somebody else; I suddenly observe myself doing this. But as soon as I become in this way self-conscious about my own *activity*, the situation as I see it, that is, the situation to which my action is adapted, changes. The situation, as viewed by an informed outside observer, has also changed, because of the additional factor of my self-consciousness. Before the moment of self-consciousness, it would not have been true to say that I was deliberately trying to annoy, although this may have been the actual tendency and the likely effect of my actions. But if I still continue on exactly the same course of action after I have become aware of its tendency, it will now for the first time be true to say that I am deliberately trying to annoy. I cannot escape the burden of intention, and therefore of responsibility, which is bestowed upon me by knowledge of what I am doing, that is, by recognition of the situation confronting me and of the difference that my action is making. As soon as I realise what I am doing, I am no longer doing it unintentionally. Any impartial and concurrent awareness of the tendency and effect of my own activities necessarily has to this extent the effect of changing their nature. In virtue of this new awareness, my action may need to be re-described, even though I continue with 'the same' activities as before—'the same', that is, when externally viewed, without regard to the intention. That which began as impartial observation turns into something else; the knowledge becomes decision.

When the dialectical movement is viewed from the other side, it appears that, if I suddenly decided to try to annoy someone, after having already acted in a way that was in fact likely to annoy him, the difference represented by my decision would be simply the new knowledge of that which I had previously been doing without this knowledge; the decision here becomes knowledge. I cannot be said to be trying to do anything that I do not know that I am doing. If I can be said to have done something without knowing it, then I must have brought about some result by my activities without having tried to achieve this result. If I know that I am going to do something in the future, I shall do it with a full knowledge of what I am doing, and my present knowledge is then indistinguishable from a decision to do it. Alternatively, my present knowledge is only that, somehow and at some time, a certain result in fact will be the outcome or effect of my activities, without my knowing at the time of acting that this result will be achieved: in which case the achievement will be unintended, and my present knowledge a prediction, based upon some inductive argument. I might have observed that, sooner or later, I always in my life find myself in a certain situation as the effect of my own actions, and on the basis of this evidence I may be certain that this will happen again, even though I do not intend it to happen. I then have a choice, in virtue of this knowledge, of acquiescing in this fatality or of not acquiescing. If I decide actively to prevent this situation arising again from my actions, I will be trying, successfully or unsuccessfully, to avoid bringing about this result. If I am unsuccessful in my serious efforts to prevent it, I will be in a position to claim that I cannot at the present time help bringing about this result. This claim may be disputed by observers, on the ground that I have omitted some step that would in fact have had the desired result. But it would certainly be true that on this occasion I had not allowed the situation to occur of my own free-will, and that in this sense, and to this degree, I was no responsible for the outcome. If I am held responsible, the charge against me is one of incompetence and not of wickedness. If I am successful in my attempt to prevent the situation from arising again, this success has shown predictions based on the past, including possibly my own predictions, to be false. I had made up my mind to try to reverse the trend, without any expectation of succeeding, and yet in fact I succeeded.

It seems therefore that it is through the various degrees of self-consciousness in action, through more and more clear and explicit knowledge of what I am doing, that in the first place I become comparatively free, free in the sense that my achievements either directly correspond to my intentions, or are attributable to my incompetence or powerlessness in execution, which may or may not be venial. Whether and under what conditions the powerlessness is blameworthy is a separate, moral question, or rather set of questions, about which very little can usefully be said in general terms. It plainly depends on the type of incompetence or powerlessness, the type of blame envisaged, on the social purposes that the verdict is designed to serve, and on the particular circumstances of the case.

A man becomes more and more a free and responsible agent the more he at all times knows what he is doing, in every sense of this phrase, and the more he acts with a definite and clearly formed intention. He is in this sense less free the less his actual achievements, that which he directly brings into existence and changes by his activity, correspond to any clearly formed intentions of his own.

It is not by itself a threat to the reality of human freedom that some close observers are able to predict, accurately and with confidence, that which a man is going to do before he actually does it. The threat arises when his own evidently sincere declarations of intention turn out to be comparatively worthless as a basis for predictions of his actions. A sincere declaration of intentions is the most reliable of all sources of information about a man's future action, if he is a free agent, which entails that he is not at the mercy of forces that he does not himself recognise and that are outside his control. This is a necessary truth. If the most reliable basis for prediction of his future actions is the record of similar people in similar situations in the past, and if his own announced decisions afford no basis at all, then he is not free to guide his own activities; he is driven by forces outside his own control. If he in fact generally sets himself to do exactly that which he had intended to do, and if he does not find his activities constantly diverted in a direction that he had nót himself designed and thought of, he is fully responsible for his actions, and he is accounted a free agent. He might be a man of inconstant purposes who often changes his mind or hesitates, as new considerations occur to him. He will still be a free, responsible agent as long as his activities at any moment are exactly as he had intended them to be a moment before, even if they are not as he had intended them to be at some earlier time. He is a free agent, in so far as his behaviour is constantly correlated with his evident or declared thoughts and intentions at the time of action rather than with antecedent conditions of some other kind.

The most powerful of all arguments against the reality of human freedom is the old argument that has been given some new basis in some interpretations of the work of Freud and of his followers. It suggests that we commonly do not know what we are trying to do, and are not aware of the tendency of our actions, in a wide domain of our behaviour, and that we can often be brought to recognise the sense of our actions only by the special techniques of psycho-analysis. A neurotic, as described by Freud, is a man who is not fully aware of, and will not acknowledge, the real tendency of his own actions, and who consequently finds that his actual achievements, the constant and forecastable effects of his actions, are generally at variance with his sincerely professed intentions. He is constantly acting in such a way as to defeat his own sincerely professed purposes, until he is brought to acknowledge that he was unconsciously trying to achieve something quite different from his professed aims. In an extended, but not unintelligible, sense of the phrase, he did not know what he was all the time 'really' trying to do, or that which he was in a sense trying to do. Because he did not know, he can be said to have been governed by forces outside his own control. The recognition and acknowledgment of them opens for him new possibilities of fully self-conscious action; he can now form plans for escaping from his obsessions. He has been brought to recognise internal obstructions to the fulfilment of his sincerely professed intentions, obstructions that he had not recognised before. A psychotic altogether fails to recognise features of the reality around him, and therefore necessarily fails to have any clear knowledge either of what he is trying to do or of the actual effects of his actions. The gap between what he himself honestly says in answer to 'What are you trying to do?' and the actual tendency of his actions is so great that he cannot be held in any degree responsible for his achievements. Freud's discovery of the nature of neurosis, which does not involve a total loss of contact with reality, is not easily dismissed from the philosophy of action. We cannot now honestly suppose that the workings of the unconscious mind are to be confined to a clearly marked range of abnormal behaviour. On the contrary, we know that its workings, if they are manifest anywhere, are manifest in a wide range of our behaviour. There is a sense in which we are often not in clear and definite control of ourselves and of our own activities, even when we would ordinarily be said to be completely free agents, if we are judged by the previously recognised criteria. But one must at least be clear in stating the principle behind these recognised criteria before one can decide how far the principle needs to be relaxed and modified in its application. It is possible to view a neurotic's helplessness in the control of his conduct, and his failure to recognise and acknowledge his unconscious aims, as only a great extension of a familiar inability to control conduct, and of failure to act intentionally and with full knowledge of what we are doing. It may be argued that there is no difference of principle: only very great differences of degree upon a scale that is more extended than we had known. The discovery of unconscious purposes may be the discovery that the occasions on which we have, to a greater or less degree, misrepresented to ourselves what we are trying to do are much more common than we had previously believed. Perhaps we were previously misled, in claiming to know what we were trying to do, by ignorance of the fact that, if on these occasions we had been examined further as the psycho-analyst examines, we would have for the first time acknowledged other purposes in ourselves. This would be not a change in the sense of the word 'intention', or of the criteria attached to the concept, but rather an empirical discovery about human purposes. The discovery of the unconscious mind, and of its manifestations, may be a discovery of a new range of facts, rather than a proposal for the re-definition of mental concepts. We discover that, applying the accepted criteria of freedom, we are less free, because less fully self-conscious, than we had previously believed. The way to another and deeper level of self-consciousness in behaviour has been opened to us.

At least two conditions are necessary for saying of a

man that he is a relatively free agent and responsible for his actions. First, that he generally knows clearly what he is doing; and this condition cannot be fulfilled unless he knows his own situation in the world and generally recognises the relevant features of the situation confronting him at any time. Secondly, there must be a comparatively wide range of achievements open to him, in which he would succeed if he tried, none of which have been made ineligible by human actions and institutions. But are these two conditions jointly sufficient conditions for saying that a man is a free and responsible agent? Or is some further condition required, which in philosophical reflection we are led to believe is never in fact fulfilled, or never could be fulfilled? This question is ordinarily taken to be the problem of free-will.

I have so far suggested that there is a necessary regress in self-consciousness. Every influence bearing upon me is added to the factors in the situation confronting me, as soon as I become aware of the fact of the influence. The mere knowledge, and the identification of, the influence is enough to turn it into an objective factor in the situation confronting me. The situation confronting me at a moment of decision may contain factors, unrecognised by me, which make the success of some attempt that I may choose to make altogether impossible. Among these factors may be included psychological peculiarities of my own, and unconscious desires and obsessions. An observer, knowing some facts of this kind about me, which I do not know, may be in a position both to predict that I will fail to achieve a certain result and to say that, contrary to all appearances, and to my own belief, I could not possibly have succeeded. It has been argued that, whenever a man does not in fact do that which it is considered that he ought to have done,

181

there is some factor, recognised or unrecognised, that made the achievement in question impossible for him. Suppose that it has been suggested that he ought at least to have tried to rescue his friend. The determinist's reply will be that there was some fact about him which, taken together with some well-confirmed general proposition, explains why it was impossible for him to bring himself to make the attempt at a rescue. We only hold him responsible for his failure to try to save his friend, because we are ignorant, as is the man himself, of the causes that would completely explain his failure. But this is unconvincing, because of the impermissible use of the word 'failure'. There is no sense in which he failed to try to rescue his friend; he simply did not try. It would be a genuine case of failure only if he had formed the intention of rescuing, and then had failed at the last moment to bring himself to take the first overt steps towards this end. Under these conditions a sense could perhaps be given to the misleading phrase 'failure to try to rescue his friend'; perhaps he had struggled with, and failed to overcome, some inner impulse of repugnance or fear. He had therefore attempted something, even though the attempt never showed itself in overt, physical movement and might not for this reason be called an attempt to rescue his friend. One cannot fail to intend to do something. One can only fail to do something. Even a man's overcoming of a psychological resistance within himself may sometimes be represented as an achievement, as a feat that he may attempt. Any action that can be represented as an achievement, as something in which a man may succeed or fail, can also be represented as something in which he could not help failing. But there is no sense in which a man cannot help intending, or not intending, to do something, and there is no sense in which it is impossible for him to intend to do something, provided that he knows what would be involved in doing it. He can always set out on the course of action, even if he knows that he will encounter difficulties at the very first stage of effective action, and even if he believes that he will in fact fail before any effective action has been taken. It may for this reason be not worth trying, and, contrary to appearances, he may have been right not to try; for he himself knew that the action required of him by the moralists was beyond his powers. If he was absolutely certain that he would not succeed in doing something, his claim that he intends to try to do it, knowing with certainty that he will fail, cannot be expressed as the claim that he intends to do it, since he is certain that he will not in fact do it. In an extreme case, an utter sceptic, who is required to try to perform some supernatural feat at a seance, may obey the instructions and in this sense may make the attempt. It still could not be said that he intended to perform the feat (e.g. to make the table turn), since he did not believe that there was the least possibility of the table turning as the result of his efforts.

Even if it is admitted that 'impossible' is a concept that applies to actions, and not to the intention that accompanies an attempt, it may be still argued that the intentions that a man forms, the attempts that he considers making, are limited by his intelligence, his upbringing, the range of his imagination. What a man will *think* of trying to do is narrowly circumscribed and may sometimes be predictable with almost perfect accuracy. The range of his thought, and the possibilities of action that have been suggested to him in his upbringing and social environment, may be exhaustively known. Even if we do not say 'He could not have thought of doing that', we certainly say 'He could not be expected to think of that'. We may justifiably say that only certain projects could possibly occur to him, and, with some intimate knowledge of the man and of his history, we can even now predict precisely what these projects would be. Looking back to an age and a culture remote from our own, we allow that possibilities of action, based on discriminations then unrecognised, were not genuine possibilities of action for those who lived at that time. It seems artificial to speak of a wide range of courses of action as being open to a man, if there is not the slightest possibility (in the sense of likelihood) of his thinking of them as possible courses of action. This objection brings in again the sense of 'possibility' that is connected with prediction, and with well-known uniformities in Nature. 'It is quite out of the question, and absurd to expect, that the idea of doing that should ever occur to him'. Or 'It is known that such men as he never do think of doing that'. Both these statements are logically compatible with saying 'He could (i.e. he would be able to . . .) do that if he chose', and yet both are in many contexts good grounds for saying 'It is pointless to blame him for not doing it'. There are many things that a man would be able to do if he chose, and that at the same time he cannot be expected to do; it may be evident from general knowledge of human nature and of his social environment that such a thought would never occur to a man of his kind, in such an environment and with such a background. It is merely a fact, and perhaps a fact that could be explained as arising from his history, that the thought and the interest in question would never occur to him. It would be a misleading metaphor to say that he was imprisoned in his own world of thought and within his own circle of interests and that he was not for this reason free; misleading, because a prison is designed to be something from which one will not succeed in escaping even if one tries, to be an insurmountable obstruction. A neurotic may meet an insurmountable obstruction when he tries to dismiss a certain obsessional interest from his mind and finds that he is unable to do it. He may therefore be said to be the prisoner of his obsessional desires, in a metaphor that is only a little overstrained. He may feel himself to be a prisoner, and feel himself unable to escape when he tries. He may feel his will encountering an obstacle whenever he tries; these metaphors seeming to him altogether natural and irreplaceable in describing his experience. But the man whose thoughts and interests in fact revolve within a particular narrow circle is not honestly to be described as imprisoned within this circle, even if we can explain very clearly why his interests are so narrow by reference to his past and to historical causes. In what sense can he be said to be responsible for the limitation of his interests and of his ideas, if we can explain clearly how this limitation arose from causes that were outside his control, such as his upbringing, his education and circumstances of birth?

Certainly there is a sense in which he is responsible, if it is within his power now to widen his interests and if he has not tried to do this. There is a sense in which a man is responsible for any condition that he would be able to change if he tried, even if the condition was originally the effect of causes outside his control. If this principle were abandoned, one aspect of the distinction between human beings as intentional agents and animals, which are not intentional agents, would have been lost. Human beings can identify their own limitations, as one feature of the world among others to be self-consciously accepted, or, if possible, deliberately changed, rather than simply responded to. They can understand the causes of the limitations of their own thought and interests, and they may either acquiesce in these limitations or they may try to change them. No consistent principle of responsibility can distinguish between positive actions and omissions: for instance, between not trying to change and not trying to preserve one's state or condition, or between trying to change and trying not to change one's state or condition. The sign of negation cannot be used to draw a dividing line, and the possibility of substituting a positive verb for a negative verb varies in particular cases from language to language. There is no general, intuitively evident principle upon which a verb that marks an action can be discriminated from a verb that marks an omission of action. If I delay in replying, this is as much an action of mine, for which I am responsible, as the reply will be, when it comes. Since human beings have self-consciousness and intentions attributed to them, they must be supposed to be responsible for every omission, as well as for every positive wrong, provided that the action omitted was not omitted because of a proved or presumed inability to perform it. Every man has a responsibility to look at all times for the best action of which he is capable at that time, and not to acquiesce in his natural and his socially conditioned limitations of thought and interest without having tried to overcome them. 'He is not the kind of man who would ever think of trying to do that, and he cannot be expected to'—this is a natural exculpating comment upon another man. The degree and kind of the exculpation will depend on the type of explanation suggested of the fact that he never thinks in this way. Does he lack the knowledge or the intelligence and is his critic requiring of him a knowledge and understanding that he does not possess and that he could not

186

have acquired by his own efforts? Or is the situation rather that he does not choose to cultivate certain interests, or to turn his attention to certain possibilities of action, although there is nothing to prevent him doing so? 'I am not the kind of man who would ever have thought of trying to do that, and I cannot be expected to'—this is an incomplete form of excuse, as it stands. The question would immediately arise—'Is there anything that prevents you and that makes it impossible for you?' I cannot in good faith say of myself, as I could honestly say of another—'For such and such historical reasons, and under the influence of such and such causes, I have become the kind of man who will always try to do so-and-so rather than so-and-so'. Does the phrase 'will try' here represent a decision or a prediction? If it is a decision, my character, as a man who will always try to do so-and-so, is something that I have chosen, and the external causes mentioned are only the favouring conditions without which I would not have been in a position to make these decisions. But my character is still something for which I am responsible, chosen from a number of alternatives open to me. If I had thought that my history, and the external causes influencing me, were in any respect bad in their effects, I could at least have tried to find the means to prevent or to minimise their effect. As soon as I have identified these influences as determining influences, I am thereby faced with the choice of acquiescing or of trying to find means of diverting or nullifying their effects. I may excuse my own past, seeing myself now as having been subject to influences that I had not recognised and that I had not brought into consciousness. I judge my own past conduct exactly as I might judge the conduct of another, except that I have a more full, intimate and certain knowledge of the considerations that explicitly guided me than I can normally have of the considerations that guided another. But this is a knowledge of my self-conscious calculations, and not of those explanations of my conduct, which might be given in terms of influences and causes, unrecognised at the time. I cannot have this last kind of knowledge without a policy, a strategy, being required of me as my response to the situation now recognised. If I speak about myself, and the influences bearing on me, in this objective and self-conscious way, whether as an excuse or in simple explanation, I can always be asked when I first recognised these features of my situation. From this moment of recognition onwards, I am responsible for changing or not changing my policies in one direction rather than another. This is one aspect of the asymmetry between proffering excuses for my own conduct and proffering excuses for the conduct of another. I can offer excuses for my own past, and I can explain my own past failures, as if I were speaking of another. I am no longer in the same position as the man who did those things, but am rather the man who understands more fully why they were done. Certainly there is a plain sense in which I am responsible for that which I did at that time, and I can never disclaim responsibility. But I need not think of myself, or judge myself, in any terms and by any standards other than those which I would apply to another. This is indeed the analogy that enables one to think and speak critically of the conduct of others with some assurance, because one is applying terms and standards that one has learnt to apply at first hand in one's own experience. We are always seeing ourselves from the outside, and with the eye of another, in retrospect. But it is unalterably impossible that we should either explain or excuse our present or future voluntary and deliberate action by referring to the influences bearing upon us, unless we are explaining or excusing in advance an expected failure to achieve that which we shall genuinely try to achieve. I can explain why I shall certainly, or almost certainly, fail to achieve an enlargement of my interests and a greater awareness of the range of possibilities open to me; and I can announce my decision to try. But if I try to *predict* that I will not try, and to give the grounds upon which my prediction is based, I shall find myself talking only of the difficulty that I would encounter in bringing myself to make the attempt. It must (logically) always be possible to try, and it must always be possible to achieve *some* extension of the range of my thought, even if this falls short of some ideal that I have conceived. Here the sense of my words necessarily changes when I speak in the first person singular. I can always without absurdity predict the ultimate direction of another's voluntary and deliberate action, and the workings of his will, either in my own thought about him or in direct address to the man himself. The prediction addressed to him may even influence the direction of his action, by drawing his attention to some features of the situation confronting him which he had not recognised before. In indicating the grounds upon which the prediction of his future course of actions rests, I may provide him with a new motive, or a new reason for acting, or for trying to act, in a way that will falsify my prediction. But this possibility of self-defeat in prediction is quite different from the recessiveness that is necessary when a man is observing himself in action.

The old philosophical commonplace, that we know ourselves to be free in our own direct experience, is a misstatement of the necessity that, at the moment of deliberate action, we have stepped backwards to review the possible ends that we may attempt to achieve, and that, however introspective we are, this backward-stepping can never be closed to us. In this sense another old philosophical commonplace—that freedom is the knowledge of necessity—can be interpreted as a recognisable misstatement of a truth. It is not true that as soon as I understand why I behave in a certain way, where the 'why' connects my behaviour with some regular and general causal pattern, I immediately become, by virtue of this knowledge alone, an exception to the causal law. It is true that knowledge of the factors that have been influencing my conduct without my knowledge does in itself open to me new possibilities of action. The mere recognition of a causal correlation between my behaviour and some external conditions is the recognition of the change that would be necessary for the behaviour to be different in future, even if the change cannot now be achieved by any decision of mine. Now I can think of the causal factors explaining my past behaviour as something that I may at least try in some way to circumvent or to some degree to counteract in future, even if I know that I shall not altogether succeed. In the metaphor that constantly seems natural, I have brought to the forefront, and within my range of vision, something that I could not even attempt either to combat or to promote, because it was working its effects in the dark. Merely grasping or recognising a general law, or a tendency to which I am subject, by itself gives me no immunity from its operation. The slogan 'freedom is the knowledge of necessity' may suggest that it does. But recognition of a causal uniformity at least is a first step towards finding the means of evading its effects by trying to alter the initial conditions, or the boundary conditions, upon which its operation depends. I may, for example, decide to avoid by my own strategies ever again being placed in the kind of situation in which, as I now know, certain patterns of behaviour, not controllable at will, will certainly re-appear. It may in fact be impossible to recognise or to understand more than a small set of the influences affecting one's conduct at any one time. It may be found experimentally that there are in fact some influences that no man can be brought to understand or to recognise when they operate upon himself. There is no *a priori* reason why men should always, or even generally, be able to see their own situation clearly and with detachment. Freudian psychology may have provided good experimental reasons for believing that sane men are in many situations incapable either of recognising or of controlling influences upon their conduct that may often be evident to others. This kind of inability to recognise, and therefore to control, influences operating upon me is an inability that I may discover in my own direct experience, when I meet, perhaps in the process of analysis, a felt resistance to following a certain path of reflection or to reviving certain memories. Perhaps helped by another, I may understand the causes of this resistance in retrospect. This retrospective understanding of my own powerlessness to direct my thoughts as I wish is helped by, and helps, my observation of others. Once I have been brought to recognise the inability and its source, I am in a position to take steps to overcome or to circumvent it, exactly as I would take steps to overcome or circumvent a physical infirmity. There is a familiar experience of finding oneself at a particular moment powerless to do what one had intended to do, and powerless not because of some physical infirmity. One meets an obstruction, a mental resistance, which, it seems, cannot be overcome at this particular moment, however hard one tries. When a man says 'I simply cannot bring myself to do it, however hard I try', we as observers cannot normally test the truth of what he says, and it is difficult in normal circumstances to agree upon means of testing whether he has genuinely tried to overcome the resistance. It is difficult also to prescribe the circumstances in which as observers we can be sure that an impulse said to be irresistible really was at that time irresistible. How do we here tell the difference between merely not resisting the impulse and finding it irresistible, between not over-coming a felt resistance and finding it insuperable? It seems that we can here only rely on the evidences of sincerity surrounding the subject's own testimony. He has his own direct experience of seriously trying. These are the cases in which we introduce the shadowy notion of an 'act of will'. This shadowy act fills the gap when we cannot specify any identifiable actions that constitute the attempt to over-come resistance.

We have seen that there is an artificiality that is almost unavoidable in philosophical discussions of action, because of the tendency to represent human conduct as a set of actions, each of which is a response to a definite situation, as a statement may be an answer to a definite question. A phase of someone's conduct does not consist of a set of actions, each clearly demarcated and unquestionably identifiable, in the sense in which a narrative consists of a set of statements, each clearly demarcated and indepen-dently identifiable. The situation that confronts a man at any particular time is susceptible of an indefinite set of alternative descriptions. We may therefore think of the situation as the agent would himself identify and describe it as being *the* situation that the agent confronts. But he may of course both misdescribe and misconceive the situa-tion in various different ways. He may suppose that there are features of it that call for action by him, when in fact these features are imaginary and not present at all. The intention that accompanies his action will then incorporate this misapprehension or misdescription. There will then be a wide divergence between the role that he has allotted to himself in his own intentions and his actual performance, even though the performance is entirely voluntary and deliberate. But the relation between thought and action is much more complicated than this, more complicated than has yet been admitted.

We have already remarked that there are two kinds of intention to be distinguished. First, I may know quite clearly what I am going to do in some future contingency, and my intention may be fixed and firm, although I would not be able to say, to put into words, exactly what I am going to do, if I were asked. For example, an actor may be entirely clear in his own mind about how he is going to play a particular scene, even though, if you asked him to tell you how he is going to do it, he could only say—'Like this'—and then proceed to play it. An artist or craftsman may often have definite intentions in the course of exercising his craft, and be incompetent and uninterested in the correct statement of his intentions. He may even justifiably claim that no words are available in the vocabulary to describe exactly what he means to do. He would need inventively to improve upon the usual vocabulary to describe the salient features of his own intended performance. Partly for this reason, the ancient Greeks were fascinated by the intelligence manifested in a craft, which they saw to be so different from the articulate and verbal intelligence of the law court and the assembly, or from the exactly communicable calculations of doctors and mathematicians. That the actor knew what he was going to do in playing the scene would emerge in the fact that, if he found himself doing something contrary to his intentions, he would immediately know (and perhaps say)—'This has gone wrong: that is not how I meant to play it'. With this one may contrast an intention of the second kind, where my certainty about what I am going to do is a certainty that what I am going to do satisfies a certain description. The most simple case is an action that is a response to an order or to an instruction that I am determined to obey. Then the whole point of my activity, as it presents itself to me, is that it should be truthfully describable as a case of doing so-and-so, where the so-and-so occurs in the order or instruction. In that case I know that that which I am actually doing is not what I intended to do, if and only if I know that what I am doing is not a case of doing so-and-so. An actor, who (improbably) had been given explicit instructions on how to play a scene by the author, might firmly intend to follow these instructions and might be indifferent to any other feature of his performance, apart from its conformity to the instructions. As soon as he realises that he is doing something that is incompatible with his whole performance being described in the required way, he will realise that he is not doing what he intended to do. Unlike the craftsman, he intended to do something that would be a case of doing so-and-so. The fulfilment of the intention passes through the words. In the first case, the fulfilment is direct.

If the intention behind a man's action is of the highly verbalised kind, then he has given himself a role in action, and this role may diverge very widely from the account that a truthful observer would give from his standpoint of the actual performance. On being asked what I am about to do, I may say that I am going to pick an azalea, since I have been told to do this. When I am seen to be picking a flower of a different kind and am accused of not doing what I said I was going to do, I may reply that I did indeed intend to pick an azalea and that picking this flower, which I wrongly believed to be an azalea, was a mistake of identification. I have not achieved that which I intended to achieve because of this mistake of identification.

These are the simple cases. In the life of sophisticated and articulate men, the interaction between the two kinds of intention is ordinarily far from simple, and it has implications that are fatal to many moral philosophies. A man may set out on a successful course of action that he conceives, and that he would describe, in terms that would not occur to another man as the proper description of the actions. The observer might be unwilling to think of this kind of behaviour as falling under this heading. Consequently he might misunderstand the agent's intention, which would be stated, if stated at all, in terms that are unfamiliar, or that are unacceptable, to the observer as a description of the performance that he sees. The agent's conception and description of his own actions may seem improper and unacceptable, not because they are simply false and involve a simple mistake of identification, but because they altogether omit those features of the actions that seem to the observer the salient and distinguishing features. Because the observer does not share the same classification of interests as the agent, and does not use the same concepts in classifying people and situations, he may misunderstand the sense or point of the agent's conduct, as this presents itself to the agent himself. In one evident sense of the words, he may see what the other man is trying to do and what his intentions are, because he will recognise success or failure in the action, when they occur. Perhaps also he could find some neutral description of the achievement intended that they would both accept as being a true description, as far as it goes. But this neutral account of the agent's intention, although not incorrect, is not the one that the agent himself would give as representing his own practical thought and the intention behind his conduct. It might not be the preferred description, which has determined his decision, in a case where one particular description of the action has been all-important in making the decision. Suppose that a man sees himself as encouraging and consoling his friend in some misfortune that has happened to him; exactly these words express his one and only intention at this time, to the exclusion of every other feature of his conduct and of his situation. The intention to do just this is not something that is attributed to him, or merely something that he would accept as a fair account of his intentions, if the account were suggested to him. Just this formula—'encouraging and consoling my friend in his misfortune'—represents the only role in which the agent sees himself, the precise, preferred description under which he acts. He has decided to act as he is acting, because he takes the injunction—'encourage and console your friends in misfortune'—as binding upon him. Suppose that there is an observer of his conduct who disagrees with him both as to what constitutes encouragement and consolation and also as to what constitutes friendship. This disagreement might not be a simple disagreement of fact, but rather a disagreement about the criteria of application for these two concepts—'I see what you mean here by consolation: but I do not call *that* consolation', 'I know how he has behaved towards you, and I do not call that friendship'. If he were asked what the agent's intentions were, the observer could truly say—'He intends to do what he thinks of as encouraging and consoling the man whom he calls his friend'. It might sometimes be misleading for him to say simply—'He intends to encourage and console his friend'— because this might suggest that the man whom he was trying to console is in truth his friend, and that that which the agent intends to do is in truth a case of encouraging and consoling. This kind of difference of methods of classification between two men may extend over a great range of their conduct; if they are both men largely guided in action by expressed principles, there is the risk that each will constantly misunderstand the actions of the other. Their methods of classifying conduct and situations may be widely different; the questions that they ask in identifying a man's actions may be quite different. Their actions will issue from the largely separated worlds of their thought into the common world of perceived physical changes. While each sees what the other is doing in his own terms, neither grasps the inner intention of the other, where the 'inner intention' is represented by the preferred description that the agent himself would give of what he was trying to do. Neither would realise that the activity that he perceives could be seen by the other as falling under a certain heading, as satisfying a certain description or as obedience to a certain injunction. These are not the injunctions that he himself thinks of, and this is not the vocabulary, the method of distinguishing and classifying actions, that he ever has in mind when he has a decision to make. In argument with a Marxist, a Liberal may be startled to find that actions of his, to which he had never thought to attach a political significance, in his sense of 'political', are given a political significance and intention by his opponent. His opponent distinguishes the domain of politics by a different criterion that reflects a wholly different way of thinking about practical questions. That which constitutes a situation requiring a political decision, the extent of the domain of politics, is different for the two men, and each of them, absorbed in his own way of singling out and identifying situations confronting him, will fail to divide correctly the conduct of the other into the set of individual actions, each of which had a distinct significance for the agent. Each will project his own principles of individuation of actions on to the conduct of the other, separating phases of activity that constituted a unity in the mind of the agent, and combining into a single action activities that the agent had envisaged under different headings. These are the familiar difficulties of an historian in finding a narrative that does not misrepresent the conduct of men whose behaviour, naïvely and externally viewed, is familiar and whose thought is unfamiliar. The elements of the narrative may fail to correspond to the successive and different phases of the activities of the men whose actions are described. Although no one statement in the historian's narrative is, taken by itself, false, the whole narrative may be a misrepresentation of the men's activity, as they themselves knew it.

The two kinds of practical intention—that which is unverbalised and that which requires action to be matched with words—are a special case of a more general distinction, already remarked, in the relation of a mind to a reality external to it. If I am expecting someone, I may be expecting someone whom I know that I will recognise as the expected person as soon as he appears, although I cannot describe him adequately in advance. The confirmation that *this* is the person expected lies in the act of recognition, and not in the fact that this person answers to some description that was available to me in advance. It is too simple to say 'But any one must know whom he is expecting, if he is expecting anybody'. The 'knowledge', which is 'being able to say', is not the same as the 'knowledge' which is the ability to recognise. Alternatively, I may be expecting the man who repairs clocks in this district, and, if there is confirmation that this man before me is the man who repairs clocks, then there is no doubt that this man is the man whom I was expecting, whatever other properties he may have. These are the extremes; with this, and with every other attitude of mind intentionally directed towards reality—hope, fear, want, need, and many others —these two extremes are possible. More commonly one finds the intermediate case, where the intentional attitude is in part mediated by a preferred description of the object, and is in part directed towards an object to be immediately recognised as *the* object of the attitude, independently of any particular description of it. That this is the situation on any particular occasion of my expecting some particular thing would be shown by the fact that neither the mere presentation of the thing itself, nor the discovery that any one description applied to it, would be by itself *decisive* in identifying it as the thing that I had expected. I may discover, on presentation of a particular thing satisfying the description, that it is not the thing that I expected, without immediately being able to specify in what respect it differs from the thing that I expected and that is in many respects exactly like it. The same confusion can occur with the objects of my fears, hopes, needs and over a great range of my emotional and intentional attitudes. That which I fear, hope for, or need may be identified as *the* thing, or as one of the things, feared, hoped for or needed, partly as answering to a certain description, and partly as immediately recognisable on presentation. The two routes to identification can often still be distinguished even when they are intertwined. The underlying distinction is between an intentional attitude towards a thing as being a thing of a certain kind, and an intentional attitude towards a thing, when the correct description of it does not enter into the person's intention.

This double aspect of intention, and of emotional and other attitudes, emerges also in the double aspect of the act of reference to a particular segment of reality by a word or phrase. Philosophers have in the last twenty years carefully studied the use of referring expressions and have tried to show why they are indispensable to the use of language, and to the expression of any kind of thought that is not wholly abstract and formal. But they have been inclined to isolate the act of making a reference to something in words from a more general account of intentional attitudes, of which this linguistic act is only one example. They have concentrated attention upon linguistic behaviour, and therefore upon the utterance of certain types of word or phrase accompanied by an intention. The actual use on a certain particular occasion of certain words, and the gesture of pointing that may perhaps accompany the words, have sometimes been taken to be all that is involved in the notion of referring to a particular thing. This is a mistake. The question 'Which of these did you mean?' is not the same as the question 'Which of these did you mention?' The use of the words, and the gesture, may have been a mistake, in the sense that, when interpreted according to the appropriate conventions, they do not draw attention to the thing about which I was actually thinking. Any conventional behaviour, including linguistic behaviour, may on occasion fail to make plain the intention that lies behind it. There is no essential difference between the intention that is involved, first, in referring to a particular thing in the course of making a statement, and secondly, the intention that enters into an action, and, thirdly, the intention that directs my unexpressed thought, or my unexpressed feeling, towards a particular thing or person at a particular moment. In each case there is the same complexity of the reference that passes through language to be contrasted with the reference that is direct and unmediated. In each case, whether of action, of feeling, or of statement, the question—'Is this the one?'—may be answered by first finding whether a particular preferred description applies to the thing, person or event indicated, or may be answered directly in an act of recognition that cannot be further analysed. Or it may be that neither of the two routes to identification is by itself decisive.

Perhaps the easiest way to grasp the concept of intention over its whole range is the way through Russell's *Theory of Descriptions* and through some of the arguments that have been suggested against the theory. One of the purposes of Russell's theory was to represent the meaning and the implications of any assertion of the form 'The so-and-so is so-and-so' as wholly independent of the particular intentions of any particular speaker on any particular occasion. The purpose could not be fulfilled. The variable intention of a particular speaker on a particular occasion cannot be wholly replaced by the expression of the intention in a constant form of words. Some intention, peculiar to this occasion, necessarily lies behind the words, and cannot be completely conveyed in them. It is a condition of the meaningful use of language with a definite reference to reality that a part of the user's intention in making the statement is not unambiguously expressed in the form of words that he uses. Something always remains to be elicited by further questioning, or to be inferred from the context of utterance, if the statement has a definite intended reference. If a speaker in the early twentieth century asserts that the present King of France is bald, it is plain that his statement, clearly and definitely expressed in these words, is not in fact true as it stands, since there is no King of France. The statement could not be true unless there was a King of France at the time at which the statement was made. There is no doubt about the meaning of the English words, and there is no doubt that the statement is not true. But there is a further question, also a question about meaning, which is not a question about the meaning of English words, namely,—'Whom did the speaker at the time mean by the phrase "The King of France"?' If this question is put to him, it may become clear, both to him and to others, that he had been so confused in his intentions at the time of speaking that there is no correct answer to the question—'To whom were you referring?' For him to point to any man and say—'That is the man I meant'—or, alternatively, for him to substitute another descriptive phrase for 'The King of France' and to say 'I meant the man who is so-and-so', would be in either case to make a false statement; he now discovers this for the first time, when he tries to find the man or to find the alternative descriptive phrase. There is no one man whom he recognises directly and definitely as *the* man whom he intended to speak about, and there is no alternative descriptive phrase which he would have been prepared to substitute for 'The King of France' and which is in fact applicable to an existing thing. These are the two routes open to him, when he tries to make clear, both to himself and to others, whom he intended; the direct route and the route through a description. Perhaps he finds that he does not arrive at any definite point in reality, when he tries to retrace his steps along first one, and then the other, of these paths. The confusion in his original intention consisted in the conjunction of the facts, first, that he was not certain that he would be able directly to identify the person meant, if he had the opportunity, and, secondly, that the phrase or phrases in which his intention was formulated were not in fact applicable to any one existing thing, as he had thought that they were.

It is also possible that he was not confused in his intentions, and that he can later give an honest and true answer to the question—'To whom were you referring when you spoke of the King of France?' Although the statement that he actually made is, as it stands, false, since it falsely implies that there is a King of France, it is possible that the person to whom he was referring is in fact bald, and that his mistake consisted in referring to him *as* the King of France, and therefore in using the description 'the King of France'. This mistake itself might be of several kinds. For example, he may be an obstinate Legitimist who habitually refers to the man, who is called by most people the Comte de Paris, as the King of France. Or he may have wrongly believed about a man whom he had met, and whom he would immediately recognise as the man to whom he was referring, that this man is generally called the King of France. If he is a convinced Royalist and Legitimist, and therefore refuses to accept the generally accepted account of what qualifications a man must have before he can be correctly described as the King of France, his behaviour towards the person who is ordinarily called the Comte de Paris will have for him a different significance. He will have allotted to himself a different role in relation to the so-called King, a role which a republican, behaving in an otherwise similar way, would not claim. He sees his own actions, and forms his own intentions, through the system of classifications that he accepts and applies. The difference between the accounts that the Royalist and the republican would in some contexts give of their behaviour towards the Comte de Paris would neither be purely linguistic nor purely factual. Their difference and disagreement might not be about the appropriateness of a name or title, but might be characterised as a more general difference of political opinion that is expressed in this difference of terminology. They could each understand the intentions of the other only through understanding the relevant differences in their bases of classifying. This would be the only way of seeing the actions of the other from the inside and in terms of the agent's real intention.

This comparatively simple and trivial case, taken from the old discussions of Russell's *Theory of Descriptions*, becomes far from simple and trivial when the example is changed, and when we consider the references that one man may make to God, and to other transcendental entities. To another man it may seem that he is referring to things that have never existed and to events that have never happened. Perhaps he understands the references; there need be no failure in communication. While understanding his friend's meaning, he may believe that many of his friend's plans and actions are founded upon a system of false beliefs about the things that there are. If a man did not know that such references would naturally occur in his friend's statements of his own intentions, he might largely misunderstand and misstate the intentions, classifying only in his own terms the actions deliberately and intentionally performed. That which the agent will say that he was trying to do—for example, to obey one of God's particular instructions will be widely different from that which the observer will say, when he gives an entirely truthful account, in his own atheistical terms of what his friend was trying to achieve.

Every literate man can be said to have an ontology, if this means that every man, who is capable of stating the intentions behind his overt behaviour, has a range of reference, more or less limited, to the entities that would sometimes enter into his practical intentions. No man can be said to believe that God exists who would in no circumstances mention God in giving an honest account of what he was trying to do. No man can be said to believe that there is no God, who would in some circumstances make a completely unqualified reference to God in stating what he was trying to do. By 'an unqualified reference' is meant a reference that does not contain those expressions (for example, 'alleged', 'talked about', 'believed', 'sought') which would cancel the existential implication of the reference. The actions of another may compel me to refer, in properly interpreting his intentions, to things and events that do not exist in fact, as I believe, and also to things that could not conceivably exist, according to the implicit or explicit philosophical principles that govern my recognition of the existence of things. I may learn to understand, and to recognise in his behaviour, what he is trying to do, even though I believe that what he is trying to do is something that could not conceivably be done, and that nothing whatever would count as actually doing it. There is a sense in which I could not possibly set out with the intention of doing what he is trying to do, because I think that the project, as it presents itself to him in his thinking, has no sense and cannot be formulated as a possibility. I might set myself to perform 'the same action' that he is performing, or to behave 'in the same way', perhaps because I had some motive for imitating him. The claim of identity, here supposed to be the identity of perfect imitation, would be entirely justifiable in some contexts, where only overt behaviour is of interest. It would be an unjustifiable claim in other contexts, where the intention behind the behaviour was in question. Suppose that it is my friend's intention to ask God's forgiveness for his sins in an act of prayer: this is what he would say that he intended to do, if he were asked, and it is in these terms, and in no others, that his impending action presents itself to him in his own thought. This is his role as he kneels. I will immediately recognise that this is what he is doing, merely by hearing and understanding the words that he uses and by watching his behaviour. I could set myself to imitate his behaviour and to repeat his words. But there is a sense in which I could not set myself to do what he is doing, namely, to ask God's forgiveness for my sins, unless I believe that God exists and that a sense can be attached to the notions of God's forgiveness and of human sin. The 'cannot' here represents a logical impossibility. I must be ready to recognise the realisation of my intention, if I can be said to have the intention at all.

In this way the habits and rules of my thinking limit the possibilities of action for me. We cannot represent human conduct as detachable from the thought that directs it, as if actions were a universal system of natural signs, always intelligible on mere inspection. We can only be sure that we will always be able to understand what a man is doing, or is trying to do, on mere inspection of his overt behaviour, if we know that he generally follows the same habits and rules of thought as we do. An action is not entirely and always transparent; so also thought is not entirely hidden, since it comes to light in statements of intention accompanying or preceding visible behaviour. We see what another man thinks can be done, the direction and limit of his calculations, and therefore we know whether in general he thinks in the same terms as we do, even if on particular occasions we can only guess what he is thinking. The knowledge that he does, or in certain respects does not, follow the same habits and conventions of thought as we do, together with observation of his behaviour, gives the basis of analogy, and the rule of inference, that enables us to say—'Since we see such movements and such an expression and manner, he must in all probability be thinking so-and-so, and he must have such-and-such an intention'. Or we may infer that he cannot have such-and-such another intention, since these are not the terms in which he ever thinks. Within a single society of men who have learnt to enter into the common conventions of behaviour and expression that are the background of a common language, systematic misunderstanding is virtually impossible. The sceptical doubt reasonably occurs at the meeting of cultures.

The limits of a man's habits of thought are limits also of what he can be expected to try to do. It would usually be pointless to censure a man for not having set himself to do something that he could not have been expected to think of doing, and that would require him to enter into a way of thinking that is entirely strange to him. Often it is the point of a moral comment addressed to a man, not that it should be censure, but that it should *inform* him of a way of viewing his situation, past or present, and of a possibility of action, that would never otherwise have occurred to him. It is a mistake of philosophers to ask—'What is *the* (i.e. the single) function of moral judgments?' and then to wait for an answer: 'They are prescriptive' or 'They are informative' or 'They express feeling'. It is a deeper mistake to suppose that there is a clearly recognisable class of utterances, which are to be called moral judgments, if and only if they are wholly concerned with the evaluation of actions. The criticism of the narrow limits of a man's habits of thought, the suggestion to him of other ways of classifying feelings or persons, may not be directly related to any specific actions of his. Yet such suggestions may still fall within the domain that is naturally called the domain of morals. The questions of whether he could have been expected to think differently, and of whether he was responsible for thinking of his situation as he did, may often be altogether pointless, or even meaningless, questions. A man's habits of thought are not to be represented as products of his will, as if he had deliberately chosen them from a number that were originally available to him. He exercises his will, and makes choices, only within the familiar habits and social conventions of thought and reference that present the possibilities open to him. He was born with a particular inheritance of conventions of reference, and his habits of reflecting upon and criticising behaviour have been as imperceptibly acquired as his original habits of behaviour. The habits of self-conscious criticism may modify the habits of behaviour. But the habits of criticism are themselves only slowly revised by further criticism and comparison, and by communication with minds that are outside the circle of convention and custom within which he is confined.

Contemporary moralists are apt to represent all moral judgments as injunctions of the general form 'You ought to do, or to have done, so-and-so', and to attach to this injunction the implication 'You can do, or could have done, so-and-so'. This is the heritage of Kant, who represented all practical thought as ending in an imperative addressed to the will. This imperative, if it is categorical, must be acknowledged to be evidently binding on all rational men as soon as its implications are understood. No place is allowed for moral inquiry, for the practical thought that explores new possibilities, that attempts new discriminations. No place is allowed for a search for an enlarged freedom of thought, which is not the freedom of the will. A man may be dissatisfied with his own conduct and with his own intentions, not because he has failed to do that which he knew to be right, but because he suspects that he is enclosed within a system of habit that does not present the varied possibilities of action open to him. His regret and uneasiness do not arise because he thinks that he makes the wrong response to the clearly identified problems confronting him. Rather he thinks that he overlooks many of the problems and that he fails sometimes to notice features of a situation, and fails to make discriminations in conduct, which would be evident to him, if he had been trained in different habits and conventions. It is not that he recognises that his rational and superior will is sometimes overcome by desire and that he fails from weakness of will; rather that he has too narrow and too crude a conception of the possibilities of behaviour and expression. He is aware, perhaps for the first time, that there are ways of discriminating and noticing differences in situations confronting him, and in manners of performance, that have never hitherto entered into his thought and intentions. He is waiting rather for a further enlightenment of his perceptions and of his intelligence, and not for an admonition, addressed to his will, telling him to behave as he already knows, in his clearer and more rational moments, that he ought to behave. The freedom that he lacks is not an absolute freedom of the will, but rather a relative freedom of intelligence. He needs a wider range of perception and discrimination. For this reason the relevant comment upon his inadequacies, if he is to be excused, is not 'He could not have acted otherwise', but 'He could not have been expected to think of acting otherwise'. He did not yield to forces and influences that were too strong for him, or encounter obstacles, psychological or physical, that he could not overcome, however much he tried. This is almost the only type of failure in conduct that Kantian moralists recognise. Rather he adhered to ingrained habits of thought and perception that altogether excluded some of the issues from consideration. There was never any possibility, in the sense of likelihood, of his asking himself the questions that might have been asked, of his realising that there were further ends to be achieved other than the obvious ones: obvious, that is, within the classifications that he applies in every situation confronting him. He may regret that he has always moved within such narrow circles of thought, and that other, and more various, distinctions in human character, manner and expression had never been presented to him. It may now seem to him clear that on countless occasions he has failed to notice many of the less commonplace and more interesting features of his own conduct and of the situations that confronted him. He had failed in awareness, because he had not the means of awareness in his habits of thought. To this extent he had wasted his opportunity of purpose and design. In many domains of conduct, he has accepted an inexpressive and lifeless routine, which does not represent his own choice and active intentions.

It is evident that the notions of *the* action, *the* facts of the situation, *the* intention, when they are too simply applied, will support the post-Kantian view of moral difficulty as always, or typically, moral conflict, together with its corollary that moral pronouncements are always or typically injunctions, a kind of modified command. It will seem that we face a plainly arranged world, an array of facts, and that we only have to decide to perform one of a number of unambiguously named and recognisable actions, ranged as possible facts before us. In questioning these assumptions, the nature of intention, as it is reflected in devices of reference and of definite description, is the first subject of study necessary to ethics, as to the logic of ordinary language. It is not enough to consider only the part that referring expressions play in utterances and in communication between men, and the conventions that govern communication. We have also to consider the thought, directed towards a segment of reality, that precedes and accompanies action. If it is true that there is a double form of intention, the intention that does not pass through the description of the action intended, and the intention that is tied to its formulation, the identification and naming of an intentional action is not simple.

'The same action' will sometimes be differently named, and have a different significance, for a man who has beliefs about the existence of things that are different from the agent's beliefs. He will not accept the agent's honest account of his own action as a possible description of any action. Each enclosed within their own systems of belief, they will not find themselves talking about the same action, although they are certainly talking about the same person and the same phase of his activity. Because of this possible doubt about the nature of the action envisaged, moral reflection is often a preliminary, not to a choice between clearly identified alternatives, but to the discovery that a possible course of action, which was originally identified under one description, could be described no less truthfully in quite different terms. For this reason examples of moral dilemmas, occurring in the writings of moral philosophers, must disguise rather than reveal the nature of practical reason. The examples are only identified through their descriptions, and therefore, however exact the description, one is confronted only with abstract possibilities. Each man will recall from his own experience examples of uncertainty in description of his own conduct: there were occasions when his own conduct had not yet assumed the plain outlines which an accurate biography might lend to it. Outside his own experience he can find examples in history: for example, Purcell's Life of Cardinal Manning is a study in the ambiguity of description of conduct, and not a study of hypocrisy. Finally, examples may be found in any fiction that tries to reconstruct exactly this density and uncertainty of experience: in Chekhov and Ibsen and Conrad, who represent their characters as looking forward uncertainly to the possible descriptions of their conduct, to their still unsettled roles.

Aristotle's account of practical reason shows the morally instructed man as *perceiving* the particular actions before him differently from the uninstructed man. The admirable man's superiority does not consist solely in the fact that he is determined, and shows himself in action determined, to be courageous rather than cowardly, noble rather than squalid, but rather in the fact that he immediately recognises in particular cases what the courageous action is. Moral instruction therefore is not so much a strengthening of the will, and an appeal to principle, but rather a habituation that turns a man's interests and intelligence in the right direction, leaving him with a true, but perhaps unstated, conception of what human life should be like. By reference to this habit of exact discrimination he assesses every situation before him. There is no notion in Aristotle's philosophy of 'the facts' confronting the agent as by themselves defining the choice before him. A man's own desires, tastes and intentions form the path that he is following and determine the alternatives before him, within the limits set by chance and natural necessity. A man's interests direct his perceptions, and his perceptions pick out the facts that are relevant to his interests.

The freedom of the will is only one part of the freedom of the mind in practical thinking, and injunctions ('You ought to do this') are only one kind of moral judgment. Every rational man must know that his own interests are comparatively confined and that he habitually views situations; and his own performances, largely in the set and conventional terms that he has inherited and passively learnt. He knows that there are many ways of classifying his own actions which would never suggest themselves to him, and that there are many features of the world around him, which he never notices; they would seem to him important, if they did happen to be marked within his habits of classification. He can come to understand the influences in his own environment and upbringing that have formed his habits of thought and his methods of classifying actions, just as he can understand the causes of the fears, aversions and impulses that are obstructions to his will. He will count himself more free in his thought whenever he is able experimentally to detach himself from his own habits and conventions of thought and to redescribe his own situation and conduct from a new point of view and in new terms. As self-consciousness is a necessary prelude to greater freedom of will, so it is also a necessary prelude to a greater freedom of thought. That I happen to have been born at this time and in that place, when virtues and vices, motives and actions, were classified in this particular way, may seem to me a contingency, which I ought not to allow to limit my own thought and to limit the intentions that I may form in ordering my own life. I cannot acquiesce in this contingency and partiality, once they are recognised, and at the same time claim that I am following an idea of a good man's conduct that has some rational, and therefore entirely general and impartial, justification. Reading history, I learn that to ascribe certain intentions, now familiar, to men living in earlier centuries would be to put words into their mouths and minds which could not possibly have occurred there. I therefore try to ensure, by reflection, that the terms in which I present possibilities of action to myself are terms that I have myself freely chosen and confirmed as the appropriate ones, and that they have not been similarly imposed on me without my actively questioning them. The choice implies that I am constantly reviewing alternative conventions of thought, and that I am always open to the suggestion of new possibilities of classification.

In this reflection there is the same effort of detachment, the same recessiveness, as we have noticed in the exercise of the will against psychological obstructions, when I try to bring myself to act against a resistance within myself. Here again the condition of being active rather than passive is self-consciousness and the recognition of a necessity, the necessity that each man is confined, in asking himself what he should do, to identifying possibilities that suggest themselves to him in familiar terms, aided by a critical comparison between his own and other principles of classification of conduct. Aware of the limits to my thought set by historical conditions, I may set myself at all times to consider my own past actions, and my present intentions, from the vantage point of other systems of thought. Having a clear intention to do so-and-so, where so-and-so represents the form of words that I would use in stating my intention, I may ask myself how this action, so identified, might be described in different ways by men who habitually attended to different features of situations and who classified actions by reference to different criteria. I would be trying to see all round my proposed conduct with a view to testing its rightness or permissibility. I wish to explore the nature and quality of the act as something that may not lie simply on the face of it, to be read off from a single description. This is at least one of the purposes of moral discussions between men, and therefore of moral judgments. In doing that which I intend to do, and which for me has one clear significance and effect, I shall also be doing other things that may be seen to have other significances and effects, when the central intention is disregarded.

This policy of 'seeing round', and of testing an intention by alternative descriptions in any difficult case, is itself a maxim of conduct, a part of a particular moral outlook. It would not be adopted as a policy by anyone who claimed to be certain that only a certain limited set of descriptions are ever relevant in deciding whether something should or should not be done. This might be someone who was following explicit instructions which he believed to be God's instructions, or who had for some other reason accepted a particular code of law as evidently binding on him. He might have decided that the whole of morality was contained in this code. He would not then be interested in any further descriptions that might be applicable to his actions, except in so far as the idea of doing certain things, rather than the mere doing them, in fact stimulated his desire. His inclination or desire to do something might be a desire to do something as being something of a certain kind and as describable in a certain way, rather than a direct desire to do this particular thing at this particular moment, without thought of how 'this thing' could be variously described. But for a man following a code of explicit and exhaustive instructions, moral issues would be matters of casuistry. He would be the type of a fanatic, because only certain already listed features of any situation would be worthy of serious thought before action. He would be governed by words, fitting words to facts, as lawyers must.

It may be objected that there is only a difference of degree between the man who makes all serious practical questions questions of casuistry, and the man who asks himself whether an action, which originally presented itself to him as an action of a certain kind, could not also be described in different terms by someone classifying actions upon different principles. Are they not both testing their decisions and intentions by asking themselves whether their projected actions could be truthfully described in certain ways?

After the early experiments of Russell and Wittgenstein, most contemporary philosophers are probably convinced that the idea of 'the facts', which are already individuated in reality independently of our forms of reference to them, is an illusion that cannot be given a sense. We divide and re-divide reality into its segments and sub-segments along the lines of our practical interests, which are reflected in our conventions of reference. Certainly we can sometimes contemplate reality, in perception and introspection, without any kind of comment, and even, with rather greater difficulty, without in any way acting or intending action, and without even an apparent shadow of a practical interest. We are then deliberately enjoying moments of pure aesthetic experience. When we are not deliberately inhibiting action, as in aesthetic experience, and are fully conscious, our intentions are always focussed on some objects to the exclusion of others, with a view to doing something with them or with a view to learning something about them. The direct intention, as of the actor, previously mentioned, who knows, but cannot say, what he will do, occurs against a background of knowledge of his situation. This knowledge *could* always be expressed in statements. But the knowledge that could be expressed in statements exists against a background of being able to recognise and to manipulate the objects referred to in the explicit statements. In a thinking being neither kind of knowledge, the direct and the propositional, can normally exist in a pure form, quite uncontaminated by the other. The actor would reject some descriptions of his imminent performance as incorrect, even if he cannot provide an apt alternative description himself. The man who intends to cook something 'exactly in accordance with the instructions in the book' will still admit that a claim to *some* direct non-propositional knowledge, relevant to cookery, is implied by this statement of intention. A man, as an intentional agent, is in this respect unlike a machine. When he intends to follow some prior instructions in his actions, that which he intends to do is not completely stated in the instructions themselves. The instructions may be complete, in the sense of sufficient, given certain assumptions about the normal capacities of men. He has understood the instructions, and to understand them is to know what actions would count as a fulfilment of them. The 'instructions' fed into a machine, designed to do the cooking, could be complete, in the sense that the 'adoption' of the instructions by the machine in itself brings about the intended achievement. Only in ritual and magical uses of language—e.g. 'Repeat these words after me: I hereby declare . . .'—can a man become rather like a machine, programmed to achieve without fail an intended effect. Otherwise the man who knows what he is going to do, in the sense that he can point to the verbal instructions that he intends to follow, must have some practical knowledge that is not contained in the instructions. He must know what actions would count as fulfilment of the instructions in the circumstances confronting him. If he had said 'I know what I am going to do', and had then repeated the words of the instructions, this claim to knowledge would be mistaken, if he proved to be wholly ignorant of the actions that would count as translating the instructions into action. The predominance of verbal knowledge over non-verbal knowledge in his intentions is therefore always a matter of degree. The casuistical ideal of blindly follow-ing the law, once and for all adopted as binding, is a possible ideal only if it is not pressed to its theoretical limit.

On the other hand there is no way of considering the nature and quality of the act intended except by comparing it with more and more groups of other actions, and by describing it in different terms and by drawing attention to different features of the surrounding situation. It may be that a single comparison, a single characterisation of it, is sufficient to show that the action is to be condemned without further questioning, as a case of flagrant injustice, for instance, or as a case of wilful persecution. The fact that the action intended could be truthfully characterised in these terms may show that it is beyond doubt wrong, irrespective of anything else that could be truthfully said about it. Perhaps I have learnt by experience, that is, by living through these things, or I have decided by reflection, that there is no other known type of conduct that is more opposed to my ideal of conduct than are those actions ordinarily classified as injustice and persecution. It is conceivable that someone might disagree with this opinion, and would suggest that other types of vicious conduct are far worse and more degrading. He may disagree, either because he has a different idea of human excellence and therefore orders the typical vices differently; or because he has experienced, or learnt of, other vices that I have not even considered. The moral argument, even at this level of generality, would always contain appeals to experience, the actual living through situations, as the instances by which the otherwise abstract ideal of conduct must be tested. But the appeal to experience must itself pass through descriptions of the situations cited. *What* there was in a particular situation, or in a particular course of conduct, that made it degrading has to be isolated in descriptions, if it is to be clear in my reflection. *That* the situation or course of conduct was degrading I may perceive directly in my experience of them, even if I cannot subsume the conduct under a heading as an already recognised vice. I need finally to isolate in my own thought that which was degrading in the conduct and in the experience, partly because I will sometimes in the future be doubtful about what I should do and I may need to call on the analogy of this present occasion in deciding. I need to identify, as precisely as I can, the feature of the situation or of my conduct which was the ground of my judgment. I cannot think about what I should do, in cases of uncertainty, except by a representation of the situation and the proposed actions to myself through their relevant features. The compounding of the relevant features represents the action to me in my own thought; I have then, through my own memory and through instruction, a warning—the only warning that I can have—of what I will find in the experience of action. A man may try to imagine and to picture to himself the various courses of action open to him, without bringing words and careful characterisation into the picturing. But he cannot in imagination alone, without some aid from conceptual thinking, *deliberate* upon alternatives: at the most he can only rehearse them. He has not in imagination, as he has in conceptual thinking, the use of tightly controlled and directed comparisons with the past and an exact demarcation of the alternatives. For this reason purely imaginative exploration of future action and performance is characteristic rather of an artist's activity, in which the benefits of exact comparison are accounted less than originality. An artist generally rehearses, or tries out, his next step, rather than discuss with himself, or with another, what the next step is to be. His thinking does not need to be conceptual thinking; he can generally rely on his own immediate recognition of rightness in his work.

In conduct a man needs a certain consistency, a sense of policy and direction, that relates one action to another in a form of life, in order that he should not be always undoing what he has previously done. He requires that there should be an answer to the question 'What has he been doing in the last year?' and not only to the question 'What is he doing at this moment?' The idea of a policy, and of some continuity of behaviour, already involves the necessity of his comparing, and therefore of his classifying, the nature and effects of his activity at different times. An artist's creative activity is essentially discontinuous, in the sense that he finally furnishes one work of art and then turns to another, which may present entirely different problems. A work of art, unlike an action, has an unquestionable individuality and distinctness. But a man's life is not easily divided into a series of separate works, each finished and complete, and it would be mad aestheticism for him to try to make it so. When therefore he wonders what he should do in a particular situation, he will not be content, as a child or an artist might be, only to imagine the various possibilities. He will want to know how the whole tract of his conduct, preceding and following this moment of decision, could be correctly classified, if he adopts one alternative rather than another at this moment. If it is not obvious to him that what he is inclined to do is a part of one single, right policy and way of life, he will want to ask himself whether this action could not be seen as part of an altogether different, and unintended, policy or way of life, when it is added to his own past conduct. Observing the behaviour of his friends, every man sees others overlooking the longer trajectory of their own conduct because of the concentration of their intentions upon an immediate future. He learns that they see themselves in one role only at the moment of action; the one description in which their intention is formulated obscures in their mind every other possible characterisation of their action in its relation to their past. They have acquired over the years a character that they did not at any one moment intend to acquire, and they have finally done something that they were never at any one time trying to do. He can observe the same blind singleness of intention in his own past, as the source of a kind of mistake which he regrets, and which is not a perversion or failure of will, but rather a failure of reflection. 'I did not realise what I was doing' may be met by 'You ought to have reflected more carefully, and you ought not to have overlooked this other face of what you were all the time doing'. Because this familiar type of moral injunction is not addressed to the will, but to the intelligence, some philosophers after Kant might say that it cannot be a moral injunction at all. But it records, or may often record, a culpable and corrigible failure of practical intelligence. This is the very type of the mistake that we are trying to avoid when we think seriously about the kind of life that men ought to lead. That moral injunctions are always addressed to the will, and not to the critical intelligence, is the conclusion only of those who think of conduct as easily divisible into a set of labelled actions and of practical choice as always choice between antecedently marked alternatives. Then exhortation, quasi-command, prescription of the right course, are all that is required from the moralist, together with an indication of the reasons that distinguish the right course from every other. No place is left for the exploratory thinking that guides action continuously in the manner and detail of the performance, and in its longer trajectory as constituting a way of life. The frequent difficulty and uncertainty in discerning the quality of a proposed course of conduct altogether disappears from view. Every action, and even the most inconspicuous voluntary gesture, can be seen as part of a manner of life, and of a set of attitudes to experience, which can be intentionally changed and controlled, when the person acting is made aware of them as finally forming a certain pattern, and as gradually constituting his character. He must unavoidably reflect upon these patterns as he guides his actions and makes his individual choices. If he has once left the most primitive level of self-consciousness, and therefore has the freedom of reflection, he cannot easily see himself as guided by any established morality that is already complete.

Chapter 4

CRITICISM AND REGRET

To recall an argument from Chapter 2: there is no constant sense attached to the phrases 'same thing' and 'same event' or even 'same action', when these phrases are taken in isolation from any context that suggests the respect of identity. Reality is not divided into units that are identifiable apart from some particular system of classification. 'Same church' and 'same building' have a sense that is specified by the sense of the concept of a church and of the concept of a building. Pointing at an object before me, I may say—'This is the same church that you saw here twenty years ago, but it is a different building; the original one was burnt'. The criterion of identity for churches is part of the sense of the concept of a church: the criterion of identity for buildings is part of the sense of the concept of a building. One might almost say of a structure that it is the same 'as a church', but that it is different 'as a building'. There are necessarily a number of these organising notions in language—'same', 'similar', 'exist', 'true', 'certain'—that systematically vary in the conditions of their application, depending on the type of expression with which they are combined. These are concepts that necessarily enter into every kind of discourse in which statements can be made.

There is another notion that is almost, but not entirely, as general and unrestricted in its application as the five mentioned above: the notion of goodness. It is less obviously general in its application, since it is not immediately and self-evidently impossible that a man might refuse to use it, or any notion that was logically connected with it, and yet still use a language normally in other respects. We are to suppose a man who refuses to praise, to criticise and to commend. He would have denied to himself one natural human activity, or rather a set of activities. The hypothesis is that he could still convey information and make true statements of fact and of logical necessity. He could still discuss with others, or review in his own mind, the various courses of action open to him and announce his reasons for choosing one course rather than another. He could even offer advice upon courses of action to others and discuss the practical possibilities with them. But he could not reflect systematically upon the reasons that guided his own actions, or the actions of another, without raising questions of good and bad actions, good and bad lives, good and bad men. He could not justify or criticise what he had done, except by saying that he had not achieved what he wanted. He could only state, in a matter of fact way, that certain considerations had influenced his decisions, and that he was in fact pursuing certain ends; and he might add that he intended always to pursue them. Deliberation would be for him an uncertainty about what he wanted, or about the necessary means to attain what he wanted. He would never express or entertain regret about his past conduct, unless to admit that he had not achieved that which he wanted to achieve is to express regret.

This amputation of critical thinking may so far seem just theoretically conceivable, if we are only supposing a man who, having in his language the means to criticise himself and other things, still refuses in fact to use any phrases of criticism or ever to think about the worth of things. The institutions of criticism, praise and commendation exist in his society. But he may be supposed to have chosen to have no part in them. But there is an insoluble difficulty in pressing the hypothesis to its conclusion. Anyone who applies concepts necessarily applies also the distintion between a standard or normal case of something falling under a concept and an abnormal or imperfect case. He cannot avoid making this comparison. A man who asks himself or another whether a particular action is a means to the attainment of a certain end must understand and accept a qualified answer of the form 'It is *a* means, but not the best means'. If he asks whether the present time is the time to perform a certain action, he necessarily understands the idea of a better time and the best time. The comparison, and the ordering of possible replies to such questions, is unavoidable. The same comparison is made when, in explaining the use of any classificatory concept, one distinguishes the standard or perfect instance of something falling under the concept from imperfect or border-line cases. The comparison and ordering of specimens as more or less imperfect specimens of a kind is as unavoidable as the comparison and ordering of statements as more or less certain. The sense of a classificatory concept is fixed by the contrast between the central and unquestionable specimens falling under the concept and the border-line and challengeable cases, as the sense of a statement is determined by the contrast between the conditions in which it is certainly true and the conditions in which it is uncertain. We could not apply concepts to our experience without making this kind of comparison. We necessarily have the idea of 'more or less a so-and-so' as part of the procedure of classification itself, and therefore as intrinsic to any use of language in thought and in speech.

It may be objected that this kind of comparison and

ordering of things as specimens of a certain species is still not the same as a comparison of them as good or bad so-and-so's. To be a standard or perfect specimen of a certain species X is not necessarily and always the same as to be a good X. This logical connection will certainly hold whenever the main ground of classification of things as X's is found in the actual or possible use of the things by human beings: then to be 'a good so-and-so' is to be 'good as a so-and-so'. But that something is a standard or perfect specimen of the species tiger does not necessarily imply that it is a good tiger. Indeed the phrase 'a good tiger' does not have a constant and obvious sense. The grounds of classification of things as tigers do not by themselves supply a constant and obvious sense to 'good as a tiger', although in a particular context this phrase may be given a clear sense. When the grounds of classification do not in any way involve the more or less constant part that the things classified play in human life, the phrase 'a good so-and-so' will not have a clear and constant sense. A determinate sense for the phrase will only be suggested by a particular context of use. This is the objection.

One may always impose a constant sense on the phrase 'a good so-and-so' by prescribing, for a more or less limited purpose, the criteria by which the excellence of different specimens of the class are to be judged—as, for example, by the judges at flower shows. These criteria will not be arbitrary and their choice not unmotivated, since they will be directly or indirectly based on the distinguishing characteristics of the species, and on the part that it plays in human life. The basis of the criteria of comparison will be the degree of development of the distinguishing features of the species: in general, the more the distinguishing features of the species are developed, the better the specimen is as a specimen of its kind. In so far as things are already classified as possible instruments for human use, the very procedure of classification shows the sense of the valuation of things as more or less good so-and-so's, without the need of *choosing* criteria of evaluation. A surprising proportion of class concepts, outside the exact sciences, in fact include some reference to normal human uses and activities in the conditions of their application. The vocabulary of common sense, unlike the vocabulary of scientific inquiry, is in this way largely anthropocentric. The use of this vocabulary brings with it the idea of comparing different things of a certain type as approximations to the perfect and complete specimen of that type. There seems therefore no possibility of a man identifying objects of use around him without also making elementary comparisons between things as more or less good or inferior specimens of their kind, and therefore as serving their typical purposes, or playing their typical part in human life, more or less well. If men were wholly inactive observers, and if the main grounds of their classifications were found in immediate sensuous similarities, comparisons of specimens falling under the same concept would not in general have the same evaluative force. 'Being a standard specimen of its kind' would not generally have the implication of 'serving its typical purpose well'.

Most modern philosophers, and particularly British empiricists, have objected to the Greek conception of the value of a thing of a certain type as being determined by the 'end' or use of this type, and of its 'end' or use as being determined by the definition of its type. They have argued that the idea of the end or purpose, that enters into the definition of any type, involves a confusion of fact and value, and that there is no legitimate inference from the definition of a type to that which constitutes the excellence of an instance of that type. They have not allowed a sense to the Greek notion of the end, or purpose, intrinsic to any class of things, except when the class is a class of artefacts designed for a definite purpose. But in looking for the grounds of classification associated with a concept, one asks oneself the question—'If one encountered a set of things exactly similar in other features to things of the kind in question, but different in this one, apparently essential respect, would one apply or withhold the concept?' The distinction between superficial and essential features, tested by supposing unreal and even fantastic examples, uncovers the point or purpose of the concept, the ultimate ground of the classification. If creatures from another planet, anatomically similar to men, were discovered, would we choose to call them men, if they had no language, social conventions and powers of thought and of expression above the animal level? Evidently not. If creatures from another planet, anatomically very unlike men, were discovered, would we choose to call them men, if they communicated thoughts and intentions in a language that we could understand? Evidently the answer would depend on the purposes for which this classification was required. For ordinary practical purposes, and if the interests of physical science were disregarded, we would classify them as men, because we would treat them as we treat human beings in all our ordinary dealings with them. They would play the same, or a sufficiently similar, part in our lives as human beings now play. The example is crude, and the essential powers which we count as distinctively human, and which would govern our application of the concept in strange, unforeseen circumstances, are immensely complex. If we decide that the capacity to think is essential to man, the word 'thought' is still inadequate to summarise the whole range of highly differentiated behaviour, of social convention and practical deliberation into which the use of a language enters as a part and as a consequence. But the complex is tightly enough knit for the phrases 'a good man' or 'good as a human being' to be constantly intelligible in ordinary speech, even when these phrases are con sidered in isolation from any particular context. We can easily place the phrase 'a good man' alongside 'a good athlete' and 'a good administrator' in the same sentence without a sense of incongruity, of having moved from the intolerably vague to that which is entirely clear. Rather we have moved from a relatively vague expression to a relatively precise expression.

When there is disagreement between two men about the criteria of comparison and appraisal appropriate to administrators and athletes, the argument will necessarily turn back to the principles upon which we classify one kind of activity rather than another kind as administration or as athletics. If the two men cannot agree on the criteria of appraisal of administrators and athletes, it must be true that they have different concepts of administration and athletics. If the argument is pressed far enough, no other possibility will be left. If one of the disputants is persuaded that he is eccentric in his classification of human activities, he will at the same time change his criteria of appraisal of men considered within these classifications. This revision of his conceptual scheme may sometimes be relatively trivial and easy, a mere matter of changing a few labels: 'I agree: perhaps it is wrong in this case to say "a good administrator": better "a good policy-maker".' But sometimes a revolutionary change of his conceptual scheme may be involved, because the dividing lines of his classifications have to be changed across a very wide band. He realises now that in his thought he had been grouping together under a single heading powers and activities which, on reflection, he wishes to hold apart as being for him, as he now decides, significantly different in their interest and in the peculiar part that they play in human life. He may have been brought to this realisation of a difference by being asked how his classifications would stand up in circumstances that he had not previously envisaged. Then he realises that the true ground of his classifications in this domain is not what he had previously thought that it was. His appraisals and comparisons in this domain will correspondingly change with his changed division of the domain.

There are some concepts that are permanently and essentially subject to question and revision, in the sense that the criteria of their application are always in dispute and are recognised to be at all times questionable. They are essentially questionable and corrigible concepts, partly because of their connection with variable human emotions rather than with disinterested scientific curiosity or with the basic needs of men as natural objects. If some of the grounds of classification are to be found in changing human desires and attitudes towards things, and in changing social forms, rather than in the properties of natural objects, undisputed and standardised criteria of application cannot be expected.

The second characteristic of essentially disputed concepts is that they are very general and abstract. The boundary of a specific concept is more easily drawn, and is less apt to be disputed, because the consequences of any change in its application are less far-reaching. Prominent among these perpetually disputed concepts are the concepts of morality, of art, and of politics. Any dispute about the boundaries of these very general concepts involves a dispute about a host of connected notions. The grounds upon which we choose to distinguish moral problems and virtues as essentially different from all other problems and virtues, or art as different from every other human product, or political activities from all other activities, will commit us to a number of consequences in the application of other emotionally charged concepts. It is always the part of philosophers—in ethics, aesthetics, and political philosophy—to chart these consequences and to show the connections, and the competing possibilities of classification, as clearly as possible.

The natural starting-point is the concept of man itself. It seems that one may distinguish that which is distinctively human from everything else in the natural order, taking a ground of classification that is remote from a biologist's interest. We ordinarily speak of 'a good man' outside any philosophical context and certainly without any biological classification in mind. 'He is a good man' is a statement that could be contradicted in the words—'He is a good engineer (or writer or politician), but he is not a good man'. The question then naturally arises—'What constitutes being a good man? And how is being a good engineer or writer or politician related to being a good man?' 'What constitutes being a good man?' asks for the distinctive powers of humanity, as we might ask for an elucidation of the art of sculpture and of the distinguishing power of this art among other arts. We shall scarcely be puzzled in looking for a definition of the concept of engineering, because the concept of engineering is too specific, too little general and abstract, to be problematical. Secondly, the distinction of engineering from other activities and interests scarcely engages our desires and emotions. A dictionary, or a scientific text-book, is therefore normally enough to make clear the essential powers and virtues of the engineer without a further dispute that goes back to ultimate principles of classification. The idea of man, and of that which is distinctively human, is of much greater generality, and, if this idea was once made firm and clear in its outlines to me, it seems that every other essentially disputed notion must fall into place, including those that are peculiar to aesthetics and politics. If most classifications of things, other than the disinterested classifications of science, have their grounds mainly in human powers and interests, the distinguishing of these powers and interests, and the understanding of their relation to each other, have an absolute priority in understanding the whole range of our thought and the structure of our vocabulary. For this reason it is possible to characterise philosophy itself as a search for 'a definition of man', and to interpret the great philosophers of the past as each providing a different account of the powers essential to men. Each philosophy marks differently the domains of reason and sentiment, of thought and perception, of will and desire, and therefore has its own definition of the intellectual, the moral and the aesthetic powers of men. Each philosophy of mind therefore provides a different ground for a stated or implied definition of the essential virtues of men.

This deduction of the essential human virtues from a philosophy of mind will be *a priori* and presumptuous, if it is not at every point guided by concrete observation of those ordinary divisions of human powers and activities which have been found useful in experience and which are already marked in the vocabulary of our language. It was Aristotle's method to illustrate his own abstract scheme of the nature of man with examples of ordinary appraisals of human activities. The concrete details of virtues and vices, exemplified in well-known forms of social life, gives a sense to the abstract and *a priori* division of human powers. Aristotle believed that the nature of man was something finally ascertainable, fixed and certain, because he held that correct definitions and classifications of things correspond to some single, eternal scheme of reality. No critical philosopher can now believe that an inquiry into the concept of man, and therefore into that which constitutes a good man, is the search for an immutable essence. He will rather think of any definition or elucidation of the concept as a reasoned proposal that different types of appraisal should be distinguished from each other in accordance with disputable principles derived from a disputable philosophy of mind. He will admit that this is the domain of philosophical opinion, and not of demonstration.

A philosophy of mind, that is, a division of human powers and their manifestations according to some principles derived from logic and the theory of knowledge, is a necessary part of any philosophy of any kind, even if it is not explicitly taken as the starting-point. Descartes, Spinoza, Leibniz, Locke, Hume, Kant, Hegel, and Russell each proposed their characteristic divisions of the powers of mind. The classification of different forms of language by reference to their normal functions in speech, which is the typical method of contemporary philosophers, is still inescapably the classification of mental activities by reference to some principles, whether explicitly declared or not. The different uses of language have ultimately to be understood as acts of communication, and therefore as parts of different forms of social life. The setting and context of use must be illustrated with a wealth of concrete detail before the lines of division in language are understood. Philosophy as linguistic analysis is therefore unwillingly lured into a kind of descriptive anthropology. The principle of individuation, by which one use of language is distinguished from another, has to be founded upon some division of human powers and activities that is external to language itself.

Any proposed classification of the activities characteristic of man, and of his powers and therefore of his virtues, contains an element of legislation or prescription. It must always be understood as one of a number of equally consistent possibilities in drawing the lines of division between one activity and another. At the last stage of reasoned argument a choice or commitment between the possibilities, with their consequences, is unavoidable. We can only appeal to established habits and conventions of classification and appraisal if, on reflection, we find reason to prefer them to every suggested alternative. The mere fact that, at this time and in this place, a certain specific division of human powers and activities has become normal and customary is not in itself a final justification of this division. When the division of human powers, of perception, thought, and feeling, was deduced from a metaphysics that showed man's necessary place in the scheme of reality, as in the philosophy of Spinoza, it was not unreasonable to claim some finality for the principles of division. But if the philosophical inquiry starts from the institution of language, as it has existed in all the variety of its forms, no finality can be claimed for any system of distinction. The nature of the human mind has to be investigated in the history of the successive forms of its social expression; the greater the concrete detail, and the greater the historical sense of its variety, the more adequate the philosophy will seem. It is not so much the dogmatism as the abstractness of traditional metaphysics that makes it now seem useless. Whether as linguistic analysis or as phenomenology, contemporary philosophy tends to find the reality of distinctions in mental life in the concrete examples with which the distinctions are illustrated.

When we criticise a man as a man, and not as an engineer or writer or politician, the criticism of him is as general as possible, in the sense that every other type of criticism of him—as engineer, writer, politician, or even as a physical specimen—could be quoted, without logical absurdity, in support or rebuttal of the most general criticism. There is no other concept, more general than the concept of man, that would be naturally used in identifying the object of criticism. 'That man (or person) is a good engineer' is a natural form of statement; but one does not normally have occasion to say 'That living thing (or 'that animal') is a good man'. We may speak of the criticism of a man as an engineer as a criticism of him in a defined and limited role. He has chosen, or he has been compelled by circumstances, to appear in this and in other roles. Any man necessarily appears and acts in a variety of roles. We can speculate about what he would have done and suffered, if he had appeared, or were now to appear, in other roles. But we cannot intelligibly speculate about his likely actions and sufferings, if he had appeared, or were to appear, not as a man, but as a god or as an animal of another species. If this is supposed, his potentialities and identifying properties, which are his potentialities and identifying properties as a man, are no longer left as a basis for the speculation. We would rather be supposing that he did not exist and that another animal, or a god, existed in his place. When therefore we discuss his virtues or defects as a man, we may be inclined to say that we are discussing his virtues and defects, simply and omitting any specific qualification; for he is *primarily* identified as a human being and not as an animal, or, on the other side, as an engineer. Yet the discussion of his virtues and defects necessarily remains within certain limits. There are many true statements of fact about him that could not enter into the discussion (e.g. that his feet are of such-and-such a size), because there is no relation, direct or indirect, that connects these statements with any statement of his virtues and vices as a man. The sense of the qualification 'as a man', if the phrase 'a good man' is interpreted as 'good as a man', is to mark the confinement of the discussion to a range of distinctively human virtues and defects. Anyone who enters into the discussion, by quoting certain facts as relevant, shows the range of excellences and defects that he takes to be the distinctively human excellences and defects. Two sides in an argument about the goodness or badness of a man cannot differ totally in the facts that they take to be relevant. At the very least they are anchored by the concept of a man to the recognition of certain activities and performances as unavoidably to be mentioned. In any case whatever, there will be a central area of common ground, even if there is no overlapping at the periphery. There is no possibility that a man's family relationships, his knowledge and mental skills, the effects of his actions on his society, his loyalties and friendships, his tendency to tell the truth, his sense of justice, his good faith in keeping contracts, should be dismissed as altogether irrelevant to his goodness or badness as a human being. There have in fact been wide differences in the weight allotted to each and all of these considerations and in the order of priority among them. But it is necessary that any human being, unlike gods and animals, lives in a society held together by conventions, enters into contracts communicates with other men and has knowledge and skills, has memories and follows traditions of behaviour, has social and family relationships. So much is the framework necessary to human life. Criticism and comparison of men must at least be a comparison of their activities and performances, in the widest sense of these words, within this constant framework of comparison. Certainly the criticism and comparison may go beyond these few essential conditions of human life; but it must include them, and any critic of men is necessarily also a man who has habits and makes decisions, governing all these aspects of his own life. As these are the permanent and distinctive conditions of anything that can be counted as human life, they are the necessary basis of the comparison between men of different periods and cultures. Relatively inessential, and detachable in a discussion of human virtue, are those activities that fall under the headings of local custom and convention, in proportion as these are altogether detachable from the essential human interests. They may sometimes be the clothing in which a man happens to be dressed, and which are not connected with the body of his essential powers as a human being. But an abstract ethics that gives a list of the essential virtues and of the powers exercised in them, is empty and almost meaningless without the details of behaviour and expression in which the changing ideals of justice, friendship, knowledge, and social usefulness are, and have been, incorporated. As the only aesthetic theory that can now be critical and enlightening is at the same time a history of changing ideals of art that points a way to the future, so the only critical ethics is a story of ideals of human excellence that at the same time points a way to the future of these ideals. It is unreasonable to reject all metaphysical deductions of the virtues, and to insist on the facts of conventional forms of appraisal in ordinary speech, without also tracing the historical development behind these facts. In default of an *a priori* demonstration of why criticism of men must assume a certain specific form, one has to illustrate its now possible forms in full concrete detail. One has to understand the facts of changing ideals, if not in a logical order, at least in an order of their development from one phase to another. Distinctively human, as opposed to animal, behaviour is from the beginning formed by specific social conventions, and the conventions of any one time are always susceptible of more general criticism when men have become reflective.

Whether a certain type of activity did in fact express some serious preference, and was in its time considered to be an essential human activity, is an historical question. Whether it was rightly considered essential is a question for philosophical decision. Whether morality, concerned with interests held to be essential to men, can always be clearly distinguished from accidents of customs and convention is also a philosophical question. It involves an elucidation and criticism of the concepts of 'morality' and 'custom'. That which would ordinarily be called custom may also be the conventional expression of a way of life that has its unquestioned standards of truthfulness, of inclination towards friendship and love, of justice, of usefulness in society, and of courage, which are the names of some of the essential, necessary human virtues. These are the words that have in fact been generally used in praising a man's activities in those spheres of activity that are common to all men and only to men. But the criteria by which men in different ages and cultures have in detail distinguished truth, friendship, love, justice, beneficence, and courage have greatly varied. A course of conduct that would in one society be counted as just and beneficent has sometimes in another society been counted as unjust and harmful, if we can allow a sense to 'the same conduct' in these altered conditions. There is still the possibility at any time of reflectively comparing and criticising the specific ideals of justice and benevolence in these two societies, and this criticism will refer to the critic's own considered standard, to his specific ideal of man as he should be. For each individual this criticism is not only possible, but necessary, if he claims to be rational and self-determining. His own criticism of himself, and the regret that he feels when he reflects on his own past, make a reference to the same standards of humanity that guide his present intentions. He has to make himself one kind of man rather than another, within the limits of his powers and of his circumstances, and the regret of something that he did in the past must be combined with an intention to avoid, if avoidance is possible, a relevantly similar event in the future. If he criticises and compares at all, he must criticise himself and compare his own manner of living with others. The standpoint of the critic and the agent cannot at this point diverge, even when he pleads an inability to avoid that which he knows to be inferior. He may intend to do something that he knows that no man whom he would call a good man would try to do in similar circumstances. He may acknowledge some natural defect, an inferiority that he believes that he cannot at this time avoid. He may find in experience that he is unable himself to acquire some, or even any, of the virtues that he considers essential to men. A reflective interest in his own character and performance, and in being a better or worse man, are not the determining factors in all his practical decisions. I may reasonably do something solely because I enjoy doing it or because I want to do it, and I may dismiss any further reflection and criticism as unnecessary. But this is only the truth that there necessarily are a great number of actions that are outside the sphere of the essential human activities on which, in my opinion, my character as a man depends. My wants and enjoyments outside this sphere, however the sphere may be defined in my judgment, are not subject to the same kind of criticism, and would never be matters for regret. This is the same as to say that they are not, in my opinion, worthy of reasoned criticism and reflection.

One of the few universally accepted connotations of the word 'moral' is 'important': no moral question can also be trivial, and not worth careful consideration. A man's morality is shown by the type of question of conduct that he takes seriously, by the type of decision about which he is prepared to reflect carefully, and to entertain genuine and reasoned regrets and criticisms. Perhaps he ponders and criticises no decision seriously, except in so far as it affects, or affected, his own pleasures. Then he is an egotistical hedonist, who considers their pleasures alone to be essential to men, even if he does not admit that he is. If I ask him why he considers his own pleasures more carefully than anything else, he may reply that the only human activities that are worth serious attention are pleasurable activities. Alternatively, he may express regret and criticise himself, as he would criticise others, for not trying to achieve the norm or standard of human conduct, as he conceives the norm. Plainly this criticism and expression of regret would not be counted as sincere, if it were altogether unrelated to future intentions. He is compelled to admit the possibility of criticism on every occasion of deciding, which is the preferring of one course of action, and therefore of one character, to another. An expression of regret is like an expression of envy, admiration, anger, fear, or hope, in at least one respect. It is not the announcement of a feeling, infallibly identified by its felt quality; it is rather the announcement of a feeling, in this case a feeling of unpleasure associated with a thought of the past, together with the identification of an object and the announcement of an inclination to behave in a certain way in the future. If a man continues to make the kind of decisions that he claims that he regrets, he could not properly continue to describe his distress as regret. He would be compelled to describe it as a vague sense of guilt or anxiety, or perhaps as an unhappy wish that he had greater powers, or that he was placed in other circumstances. 'Do you regret that decision?' is a question that requires me to *think*, and to think practically, about the decision, and not merely to inspect my feelings.

The types of conduct about which any one man reflects carefully, whether in advance or in retrospect, must fall within a more or less narrow range. His thought and reflective intentions cannot be simultaneously directed towards every mentionable aspect of his behaviour. It is a logical necessity that he must neglect something in the infinite range of human expression and activity; and almost certainly he neglects some discriminable facet of action or reaction that others have deeply considered in their ideal of human life. He has purposes, and to have purposes is necessarily to concentrate intention, and to exclude some facets of conduct from thought. His purposes may harden into habit and heedlessness, when comparison and reflection die in him and his intentions are fixed, always formulated in his own mind in the same narrow set of terms. Morality as exploratory thinking, as an unresting awareness of that which he is neglecting in his intentions, may disappear, and with it the comparison and criticism of competing ideals of human behaviour on the occasions of decision. He may cease to notice anything in his own conduct that has not already been included in his intentions. This is the unreflecting state of a morality left to itself. It is a morality without perpetual regret, because it is without any sense of the many possibilities lost, unnoticed. Intellectually and philosophically, it often rests on a naïve confidence in established classifications of specific situations, actions and mental processes as being the permanently obvious and self-justifying classifications. It cannot for long survive, when men have once become self-consciously aware of the influences, peculiar to this time and this place, that have formed their more specific habits of classification and when they are thereby driven to wider comparisons, and are therefore driven into philosophy. Finding their own standpoint limited and partial, they will try to find some more generally valid ground for their conception of human capabilities and of the essential human virtues. If they can no longer believe that this justification is to be found in any final insight into the nature of man, they may look for a justification in some interpretation of the known historical development of moral ideas, of which their own moral beliefs are a part. Then it may seem intelligible within the pattern of development that exactly these moral ideas should emerge from an earlier morality at this time. Their philosophy of mind will be a theory of the order of development of human powers with their corresponding virtues, and not a theory of their unchanging constitution. Metaphysical deduction may be replaced by a study of the successive forms of social life, and of the typical processes by which one form of social life, with its corresponding moral ideas, is typically transformed into another. But in their own conduct and in their political loyalties they still have to make a decision between competing specifications of the essential human virtues, even if they believe that the possibilities now open to their decision are not the only possibilities and that unpredictable possibilities, connected with new forms of life, will be presented to men in the future.

We cannot avoid admitting that the division of intellectual powers, the theory of the emotions, the classification of political forms, the canons of art, are in our time in need of criticism, not because previous philosophers have made mistakes in their analyses, but because the subject-matter under consideration has changed. The ambitions and methods of mathematicians, physical scientists and artists have changed and expanded, and the concepts of mathematics, of scientific theory and of art, have not remained constant. No philosophy of mathematics, science or art, however general and abstract it may be, can be eternally valid. The rejection of metaphysical deduction, and the study of the details of linguistic usage, are sometimes supported by the suggestion that all earlier philosophers have been mistaken about what philosophy is, about its necessary and permanent nature. This is an inconsistency. If we have no final insight into the essence of man and of the mind, we have no final insight into the essence of philosophy, which is one of men's recognisable activities: recognisable, both through the continuity of its own development, each phase beginning as a partial contradiction of its predecessor, and also by some continuity in its gradually changing relation to other inquiries, each with their own internal development. A philosophy may be adequate to a certain phase of human thought and it may inventively foreshadow some developing phase of art or science. Thereafter some of the work will need to be done again. Particularly the range of the emotions, feelings and attitudes of mind, identified and distinguished from each other, changes as the forms of human knowledge develop. We identify new emotions and attitudes that have never been recognised before. With a new self-consciousness, and with the extended vocabulary that goes with it, we discover new motives for action and new objects to which practical intentions are directed. A reflective man is aware that he would have recognised, and acted from, other motives in himself if he had been born and formed in other circumstances, and that he would sometimes have found other ends of action in the now differently identified emotions and attitudes of others. He cannot refuse to notice that the particular concentration that is characteristic of his own purposes is partly a contingency, something that has happened to him, and not an action of his own, when once he understands the causes of this concentration. He cannot then choose to remain confined within the circle of his customary intentions, unless either he abandons any claim to rationality or finds by continual comparisons that his habits have some philosophical ground.

A morality 'left to itself' will survive unquestioned only if it is insulated from any serious experience of art: this is indeed part of the significance of the phrase 'a morality left to itself'. Experience of art is by definition an experience in which practical interests, and the ordinary classifications that reflect them, are for a time suspended in an unpractical enjoyment of the arrangement of something perceived. Any strong aesthetic experience is necessarily an interruption of normal habits of recognition, a relaxing of the usual practical stance in the face of everything external. It is therefore a disturbance, because it is a temporary refusal to classify usefully, and to consider possibilities of action. Men are not only capable of aesthetic experience. They are also from the beginning capable of making works of art and of enjoying them as works of art. Aesthetic experience is a necessary part of any enjoyment of a work of art; but it is not the whole of it. A work of art is also enjoyed as a form of communication between men, as an expression of feeling and as a celebration of some facet of experience. It is enjoyed also as the disclosure of a person's, or of a group of persons', thought and sentiment exactly conveyed in a distinguishing style. The interests that can be distinguished in the enjoyment of art are never simple, when the enjoyment is prolonged and occupies a large place in the life of a man or of a society. At least part of the importance of works of art in human experience is that they are surprising. Any considerable work of art is in some respects an invention and must seem in some respects unforeseeable. That human beings are at all levels of culture capable of producing and enjoying works of art ought not to be accepted as a contingent fact, unrelated to their other essential powers of mind, to their capacity to form societies held together by conventions and to speak a language. Men altogether without art, like men who never dreamed or played or pretended, or who never entertained wishes that they knew to be unrealisable, would be men in a state of nature, more like animals than men. A transcendental argument, of the kind that Kant and Hegel attempted, is always needed to show the necessary connections of art with morality and with positive knowledge, and thereby to show its necessary place in the development of individual minds and of human societies. We at all times need a complete view of the necessary interrelations of distinct powers of mind. The weakness of empiricist philosophies at the present time is that they detach aesthetics, as they have detached ethics, as an autonomous domain, only contingently connected with other interests. They postulate a special and self-revealing type of experience which is subjectively recognised to be unlike any other, and is taken to be the ground of a special type of judgment, logically disconnected from every other. The enjoyment of art, and art itself, is trivialised, as a detached and peculiar pleasure, which leads into nothing else. Its part in the whole experience of men is then left unexplained.

Human creativeness in art prevents the recognised varieties of feeling, and established conceptions of the mind, from ever hardening into a final pattern. There are always surprises, the identification of new attitudes and states of mind through freely invented works of art that seem an exact expression of them for the first time. Any closed morality, so far left to itself, is always threatened with this unpredicted shock and disturbance, which suddenly illumines another possibility of human feeling and desire through the invention of a new form of expression. Without these unexpected achievements we should be left to acquiesce in some much narrower and more static conception of possible human attainment and of possible discrimination. They add another dimension, that of the unpredictable and uncontrolled sources of change in our perceptions and attitudes, and in our idea of men's normal powers. It is characteristic of any considerable work of art that its interest cannot be exhausted in any plain statement of the artist's intention. He always does more than he could previously have said that he was doing. The artist's intention is not clearly detachable from the actual performance to the degree to which it is in any uncreative activity. The power and quality of the work is only known and understood in retrospect, often after many years. For this reason good intentions in art do not have the interest and value that they have in normal conduct. The intention must be to some degree fulfilled before it is even recognisable. The idea of original art is the idea of an achievement that goes beyond any previous intention, and that must always be to some degree unexpected even by its maker. Even the most confident moralist must know that, sheltered within his own framework of thought, there are many potentially interesting features of behaviour and of feeling which he has not the means to notice. At some time they may be brought to the surface and, through the invention of forms of expression, recognised for the first time. If he reflects, he will acknowledge that these possible revelations must be infinitely many.

Since the concept of mind is, for the reasons given, necessarily an open and always disputable concept, men can only learn, in their own experience and in the history of art, morality and custom, all that has reasonably been included among the specific forms of human virtue. In history, in the arts in their different phases, in political programmes and among his friends, any reflective man will find more or less explicit projects of enlarging the current notions of human excellence. He will find varying and connected criteria of justice, intelligence, friendship, social order, and a philosophical foundation for these criteria in a theory of knowledge and of human capacity. These criteria, together with their philosophical foundation, can be made part of the material of history as a study. A common centre of meaning, and common conditions in the criteria, persist with the persisting idea of that which is distinctively human. But the more specific conditions in the criteria of application of such terms as justice and friendship change, as the conditions of social life in which they are applied change. For this reason any theory of the virtues is either wholly abstract, or it passes sooner or later into the museum. This is the solid ground for saying that, if philosophers are elucidating only the most general and abstract concepts in our language, they cannot at the same time be confident legislators and moral instructors, as the public are always demanding that they should be.

In his own action, and in the use of practical reason, a man is always forming a pattern of behaviour, and therefore a character, and at the same time criticising and regretting his own behaviour and habits in retrospect. There is therefore a circle of criticism and decision, of reflection and action, that continues as long as he is conscious. If a moral philosopher concentrates attention on criticism apart from decision, or on decision apart from criticism, he unfailingly arrives at a false conception of moral judgment. Deliberation, and choosing between alternative courses of action, is the process of criticising the envisaged character that one would assume, if one realises one possibility of action rather than another. Adverse criticism of oneself as a man is an expression of regret that one did not act in some specific way that now seems the right way for a man to act. Moral criticism of another, disapproval, whether expressed or unexpressed, is the thought that he did not try to act as a good man would have tried to act, in his circumstances and with his powers, together with the thought that one would have regretted acting as he acted, given his situation and his powers. That which I regret in myself would be in others an object of my disapproval, if they possessed sufficiently similar powers and were placed in sufficiently similar circumstances. That which I disapprove of in others would be in myself an occasion for regret. If I say that I know that I shall regret doing that which I am about to do of my own free will, I must admit, for the sake of consistency, that I would regret not doing it even more. There is something involved in the action that I know that I shall regret. But there is something of which I think that I would regret the loss, now or in the future, even more, if I did not do it. It would be unintelligible, an unserious play with words, for a man to say that he has decided to do something that he knows that he will, now and always, regret doing, absolutely and without qualification.

It will still be objected that criticisms of men, and self-criticism and regret, are of many different kinds, and that moral criticism ought to be clearly distinguished from other kinds. But what is the purpose of drawing the distinction? Is it merely an interest in the word 'moral'? Certainly there seems to be a reasonable demand for more than a clarification of a word, if the word 'moral' is defined by the following two conditions, taken to be jointly necessary and sufficient: and these are the two ideas, and perhaps the only two, generally associated with the word in all its ordinary uses: a moral excellence or defect is a human excellence or defect that is (1) important and worth serious attention, not trivial, and that (2) it is attained by the working of the will of the person to whom it is attributed, or (in the case of a defect) would be avoided if the person to whom it is attributed tried to avoid it. The second condition could be made less strict: 'a moral excellence is a human excellence that can in fact generally be attained by persons who try to attain it'. Taking the first, more strict formulation, that quality which is a moral excellence or vice in one man would not be a moral excellence or vice in another. Strictly speaking, one could not ask of a disposition, considered abstractly, whether it was a moral excellence or not; there would only be the question whether the disposition was ever or often a moral virtue in someone. This less loose formulation seems preferable, since a moral virtue is essentially a disposition that a particular person possesses. Stupidity of a particular kind may in one man be counted as a natural defect, on the ground that, when he seriously tries to avoid acting or thinking stupidly, he invariably fails. In another man, it may be a moral failing, since it becomes plain that when he tries to avoid acting stupidly in this way, he succeeds: he has not tried, or seriously intended, to change his conduct. According to this definition, it must be a matter of opinion whether a particular virtue or defect is in a particular man a moral virtue or defect. It is always a matter of opinion whether a praiseworthy disposition is an important human virtue, and generally, though not always, it is a matter of opinion whether the person in question would in fact acquire, or would have acquired, the virtue if he tried, or if he had tried.

But the difficulties of this account of the sense commonly attached to the word 'moral' are evident. What is the status of the opinion that a certain human excellence is important and is worth serious attention and is not trivial? Plainly it cannot be admitted to be a moral judgment in the sense defined, without circularity in the definition. Yet the contrast between the important and the trivial is the contrast between that which is worth prolonged thought and effort and that which is not worth prolonged thought or effort. A judgment of the value of different human activities is being made when this contrast is applied. There is nothing that is logically absurd, for example, in the opinion that creative genius in the arts or sciences is intrinsically more important, and more characteristically a human excellence, than any other virtue. A man might believe that creative ability in the arts is supreme among human virtues, simply considered as a virtue, and express this by saying that it transcends in importance any of the moral virtues, that is, than the considerable virtues that may generally be acquired by the exercise of will. From this, as from all other, ultimate judgments of the value of human powers and activities, practical conclusions can be inferred; for example, that it is always right to protect and foster creative genius, even at a very great cost in the neglect of other potentialities. It must remain an arguable question whether those human excellences that can normally be attained intentionally, by effort and by practical reason, are to be considered of supreme value, just because they are so attained: whether the exercise of will, and whether good intentions, are the most noble potentialities of men, as they have often been thought to be. As the moral excellences are often taken to be the only important excellences that can normally be attained directly by those who are persuaded to try to attain them, there is a natural tendency to represent them as the most important of all human excellences, if only as a device of persuasion. The human virtues that are not moral virtues are not subjects for direct exhortation and persuasion. The practical injunctions that follow from the recognition of them are comparatively indirect; they are injunctions to produce the favourable conditions in which, when these virtues exist, they will not disappear or be neglected.

These judgments of the relative importance of different human excellences may correctly be described as 'ultimate', in the sense that they are not always and necessarily to be derived from any one already identified class of propositions constituting the evidence on which they must be based, or the premises from which they must be deduced. They may be called 'ultimate' also in the sense that they are of the greatest possible generality and abstractness. If they are ultimate in both these senses, it still does not follow that no reason *can* ever be given for rejecting one ordering of human attainments and for accepting another. On the contrary, it is almost certain that anyone believing that the virtues attainable by the exercise of the will are the supreme virtues will find the grounds of his belief in a philosophical doctrine of freedom as the distinguishing feature of men: and he will interpret freedom as the exercise of will in practical decision. He might have interpreted freedom, as the distinguishing feature of men, as that power of reflection which enables men always to detach themselves from their own motives and intentions, and to look for some further ground for their decisions. If he takes the highest excellence of men to be the exercise of critical thought, he will be governed in his own conduct and criticism by a rather different specific ideal of the best form of life for men. We do not naturally reflect in these wholly abstract terms on the ordering of human excellences apart from a particular choice that has to be made, or can be envisaged, between one kind of life and another. The choice, and the philosophical argument that lies behind it, are forced upon us when we compare political programmes that will encourage one kind of virtue rather than another through education and rewards. Certainly anyone who has the idea of transforming society by political action must in consistency have in mind an order of priority among human activities, and therefore a specific norm or standard of human excellence. If in the course of argument and reflection it is suggested that supreme value is to be attached to a disinterested intention, or to the will to do what the agent considers to be right, we cannot avoid a strictly philosophical inquiry into the nature of intention and the meaning of 'the will'. This inquiry is a demand for a philosophy of mind that fits these concepts into a clear and consistent scheme. Whatever human powers and activities are mentioned in a statement of ends, a philosophical inquiry would be necessary to ensure that the implied distinctions are clear and consistent. The idea of the will, and of its relation to practical reason, may gradually seem less clear, and the expression may even seem totally inapplicable, to a man who had always *thought* that he understood clearly what he meant by it; he may have thought of himself as attaching supreme value to 'the will', without ever having reflected upon the variety of its possible meanings. This is the point at which linguistic analysis, the detailed study of a whole range of idioms together with their normal contexts, is of the greatest value in philosophy. A philosophical inquiry may disabuse a man of his belief that the exercise of the will, or of some other human power, is of supreme value, by making him doubt whether this familiarly named, but abstract, power is in fact clearly identified in his ordinary speech. The nomenclature that he has been using, and that has entered into his thought whenever he has considered ultimate judgments of value, may be shown to be systematically confused when confronted with a variety of different situations. He realises that the grounds of distinction between the different mental powers, as they are conventionally named, are different from what he had supposed. He has therefore been in error when he has said to himself, or to others, that he attaches supreme value to virtues associated with the exercise of the will, or to creative ability. It may even be found that there are no expressions in the ordinary vocabulary, naming powers of mind and virtues, that do exactly convey his intention. He may find that the vocabulary that he has accepted without question rests on a central distinction that he cannot in detail sustain. Then he will be compelled to adapt the vocabulary to his own purposes and to find new uses for some familiar expressions. At least one commonplace notion of a moral virtue, just discussed, combines two elements that cannot be consistently combined. Yet I might well have *thought* that I had a clear notion of a moral, as opposed to a natural, virtue, and of a moral problem as opposed to other kinds of problem, and I might have confidently invoked this distinction in justifying to myself or to others a practical decision: for example, a political decision that was grounded on the supposed freedom of the individual in purely moral questions.

It is the constructive work of a philosophy of mind to provide a set of terms in which ultimate judgments of value can be very clearly stated. At the present time any reflective person is driven to correct, or at least to re-examine, the ordinarily accepted classification of the powers of mind. More of human conduct than we had thought, and aspects of it that we had not expected, may be outside the possible control of practical reason; less of human conduct than we had thought may flow from an unalterable natural endowment. Perhaps even our ideal of what human beings might at their best become, if every now recognised possibility were realised, may be changed by this new knowledge. New positive knowledge may suggest not only new means of improvement but even new kinds of improvement, new virtues. The opinions that distinguish the greatest human achievements from the lesser are always in principle corrigible both by philosophical inquiries into the present application of the concepts and by new positive knowledge about men. The conclusions of philosophy itself, and in particular of the philosophy of mind, are always within the domain of opinion and not of knowledge. They are essentially provisional. This defect of knowledge is not on the same level, or of the same kind, as ignorance of the ultimate constituents of matter or of some other feature of the natural order. As the knowledge that we may have of our own mental powers is reflexive knowledge, the object of knowledge and the knowing subject change and extend their range together. New psychological knowledge, perhaps bringing new power to control and direct the mind, may in itself enlarge the possibilities open to practical reason. It is not an accident, an unpredictable contingency, that the new positive science of human conduct, psycho-analysis, has not taken the standard form of an experimental natural science, and that it is founded upon a peculiar form of memory and a peculiar form of self-consciousness in the subject. It might even have been predicted that it must take this form, if it is to be knowledge that explains to the subject why he has the purposes that he has. As an applied science, psycho-analysis identifies the increasing freedom of the agent to control his own conduct and states of mind with an extended self-consciousness, with a capacity to recognise in memory motives and purposes that he had not recognised before. Psycho-analysis therefore provides a reflexive knowledge of the workings of the mind that fits into the philosophical definition of freedom in terms of self-knowledge. We become aware, through knowledge of the history of our culture, of the sources of our moral and aesthetic opinions, and, in the detachment that this knowledge brings, may recognise their partiality and contingency; we have in fact adopted these opinions and attitudes as our own, but still they do not seem to be wholly ours, freely chosen upon some general grounds from every other possible opinion. So we may become aware of unconscious motives and purposes that make our past decisions and intentions seem so much less freely chosen. Rationality, and a choice between alternatives that is genuinely one's own choice, presupposes a full knowledge of the hitherto unrecognised causes of the confinement of one's choice to a particular range of possibilities. *Complete* rationality and *full* knowledge of every possibility open to us are an ideal limit at which we never in fact arrive and never could arrive. There are always the limits of our own language and culture, and of our own interests formed by social circumstance, which provide the material of reflection. We cannot suppose a man who is totally detached from every confining interest and equally open to every possibility in his thought. His self-consciousness must always operate upon a given material, the material of his own language and of its social background, and it could not operate in a void. But everyone has had the experience of coming to view some of his interests, previously accepted as inevitable, with a new detachment, as material upon which his own deliberate choice can operate. Recognising the sources of these interests, clearly identified for the first time, he confronts a new situation and has the means of deciding whether he should accept or, if he can, reject them.

It may still be objected that there is no logical necessity that we should take the notion of a good man as the starting-point in any discussion of that which is supremely valuable, and of the order of priority of human virtues: or even that the concept of virtue should be the starting-point of discussion. That which we may intelligibly praise, and praise absolutely and without qualification, may belong to a number of different categories. The principles of logic are principles of inference, and there is no principle of logic that prescribes the starting-points of inference in ethics or aesthetics. They only prescribe that, *if* we speak of the goodness of a man, we are speaking of a type of excellence or virtue that falls within the range determined by the powers that distinguish a human being. It may be argued that there would be no logical contradiction in maintaining that the absolute value of art or science or philosophy is not to be derived from the excellence of men as men, but rather that the reverse is true. Anyone who accepts such a philosophy can be expected to explain why art or science or philosophy are in themselves of supreme worth apart from their relation to human beings. He may believe, for example, in some supernatural reality which can be approached only by art or science or philosophy, and he may believe that the mundane life of men is in some sense 'unreal' or transitory or trivial in comparison with this reality. This was Plato's doctrine: in comparison with the timeless realities 'human life is not a great thing'. The goodness of a man is to be derived, directly or indirectly, from his relation to supersensible and timeless realities. But if one had been convinced that any statement referring to supernatural realities as existing things was always and necessarily void of content, one would be driven back to find within the natural order the things that are the most highly valued for their own sake and apart from their relation to anything else. It seems *logically* possible that the subjects primarily valued should be natural objects, or some arrangement of natural objects other than men. It also seems logically possible that a good state, or a good society, should be the primary subjects of ultimate judgments of value, and that the goodness of men should be derived from them, rather than that the notion of a good society should be derived from the notion of a good man. All these opinions seem logically possible and some of them have in fact been held. But they have to meet one purely philosophical objection, which is equally an objection to Platonism, to any similar transcendental philosophy, and to any philosophy that attaches value primarily to natural things. The distinctions that are marked in the vocabulary of any language are the distinctions recognised by men. 'A good so-and-so' is a form of phrase that derives its sense from some grounds of classification chosen by men for their own purposes, and from the criterion of value that is more or less directly derived from these grounds of classification. However resolutely we may try, as philosophers, to separate judgments of value from any limiting human interests, we can never altogether succeed. The human interests are included in the formation of the concepts to which the evaluative epithets are attached. Even the Platonic Forms are distinguished from other entities by the kind of human knowledge of which they are the objects. Their characteristics—they are timeless, always the same, supersensible —are directly derived from the characteristics of the most excellent human knowledge. For this reason Plato's own ultimate judgments of value can be re-stated as Aristotle in fact re-stated them: namely, that the supreme virtue of man is the habit of using the most pure intelligence upon its proper objects; his virtue is to become a pure intelligence, as far as is possible within the limits set by Nature. To attach value to any natural or supernatural entity is necessarily also to single out a human virtue, which consists in the habit of recognising these entities and in some form of active respect for them. Therefore any philosophy, that includes ultimate judgments of value, necessarily contains also a criterion of human virtue implicit or explicit, even if it is intended not to be in any obvious way anthropocentric. If a man attaches supreme value to natural processes that are not distinctively human activities, and that are not mental processes, as D. H. Lawrence sometimes did, he still has to explain how these processes are to be recognised, encouraged and enjoyed by human beings. He cannot avoid saying how the human mind must be directed, if we are to achieve some contact with that which is ultimately valuable, even if this direction of the mind is to be the suppression of critical intelligence. Similarly, a theist who believes that everything that is valuable is made so by the will of God must still suggest how the will of God is to be recognised and realised. The cultivated capacity to recognise God's will, and the habit of following its directions, must be for him the supreme human virtues, and everything that contributes to these virtues must be derivatively valuable.

This is the necessity that any judgments of ultimate value inevitably allot a sense to the phrase 'a good man', either directly or by implication: directly, if the exercise of a human capacity, whether of will or intellect or feeling or imagination, is held to be supremely valuable and worth pursuing, and if the conception of the good man is taken as the starting-point of discussion: by implication, if something other than a good man, whether a natural or supernatural entity, is taken to be valuable and is taken as the starting-point of discussion. It may therefore seem unimportant whether a moral philosopher, or a moralist, adopts one use of the word 'good' as the primary use rather than

R*   259

another: whether he claims, as G. E. Moore claimed, that the word 'good' can be intelligibly used without any accompanying empirical concept that specifies its sense more exactly: or whether he argues, as many contemporary philosophers argue, that the word 'good' is always, and across the whole range of its uses, simply the most general adjective of praise, and is otherwise wholly unlimited in the conditions of its application.

These claims about the proper uses of the word 'good' may be either accepted or rejected as philosophical theses within a general classification of terms and of types of statements; and one or other of them may be shown to be incompatible with certain facts of actual usage. But do these philosophical theses by themselves entail either that certain criteria *must* be, and that certain criteria *cannot* be, relevant in discriminating a good man from a bad man? Or is any such philosophical characterisation of the word 'good' compatible with any account of the criteria appropriate to the phrase 'a good man'? The answer to the second question is 'no': to the first 'yes', but a qualified 'yes'. Any philosophical characterisation of the word 'good' suggests a procedure by which we are to decide whether judgments of the goodness of something are to be accepted or rejected. By claiming to distinguish a use of the word 'good' in which it may stand for a simple and non-sensible quality of states of affairs, and by claiming to distinguish this use from all other uses, G. E. Moore certainly suggested to himself and to others that the ends of human action, and therefore the range of the essential human virtues, can be made evident beyond doubt to some inner eye of the mind. According to Moore, one should simply ask oneself what features of states of affairs are intrinsically good, and good without qualification, a quality that they can immediately and finally be seen to possess when one reflects. No place therefore is left for anything that can be called deciding upon the criteria of excellence of men as men, or for acknowledging the possibility of alternative criteria within certain limits, or for practical experience and observation continually influencing such a decision. The unchanging ends of human action and of social policy can be fixed with absolute finality at any point in human history, provided that men are capable of reflection and abstraction. No place is left for the discovery of new ends of action, as new powers of mind and new forms of human association develop. Similarly, a philosophy that represents the word 'good' as simply an adjective of praise and commendation, and that sharply distinguishes praise and commendation from informative speech, suggests that the acknowledgment of a power or habit as a virtue is simply a wilful act of praise or commendation. It implies that there are no limits, other than psychological limits, upon the powers and habits that can properly be included among human virtues. The decision about the essential virtues of men is only an act of will, or perhaps an expression of feeling, and is not to be restrained by any conceptual necessities. The analogy that might be thought to extend to every use of the word 'good', as necessarily an adjective of limited comparison, is repudiated. The only analogy between a judgment affirming goodness of someone as a man and a judgment affirming goodness of something of some other kind is to be found in a common act, or attitude, of praise and commendation. Both of these philosophical characterisations of the use of the word 'good' suggest specific procedures of deciding questions of ultimate value. These procedures are unlike that which is suggested by taking the idea of a good man as primary, when the word 'good' is interpreted as qualifying 'man' exactly as it qualifies 'engineer' in the phrase 'a good engineer'. If all discussions of ultimate value start from this point, they will be from the beginning confined to the potentialities of men, as thinking beings, in the actual historical conditions that now determine, or that are likely in the future to determine, their forms of association and the development of their powers of mind. Every question of morality and of public policy is then forced into this mould, and is seen as implying competing ideas of what men should be in the future, and therefore as implying some ordering of their known potentialities for intelligent activity. A consistent philosophy holds a scale of the virtues already recognised as characteristic of the good man, or of a human being who fully realises the potentialities of human beings, as a background to every moral argument and to every political decision. Those who, following Aristotle, take the notion of a good man as the starting-point of ethics will assess societies and governments as directly or indirectly producing or destroying the conditions in which the essential human excellences are attainable. 'What powers and habits will be fostered, if this form of government rather than that is instituted?' 'What kind of man, exercising some of his powers at the expense of others, is likely to be found in a social order of this kind? Is there another social order, attainable under present conditions, which would encourage or permit a greater development of the essential human virtues?' Some questions closely corresponding to these must unavoidably arise within every analysis of ultimate judgments of value and of the moral judgments entailed by them. But they do not necessarily arise in this form. A utilitarian, for example, may claim to know that certain states of mind are intrinsically good, and that nothing else is intrinsically good. He may support this claim with an account of how such judgments can be known to be true, and of how knowledge of this kind is different from, and related to, knowledge of other kinds. Within his philosophy, political decisions, in common with every other decision, are to be judged solely by their efficiency in producing and preserving the states of mind that are independently known to be intrinsically good. The form of words used by this utilitarian philosopher in criticising political decisions and institutions would not be simply paraphrasable in the alternative terminology, which mentions only the essential virtues of a good man. Something more than a difference of terminology would be involved in this philosophical disagreement; and this something more could not be represented as solely a difference of opinion about the proper ends of human action. Two men who held different opinions about the specific states of mind that are intrinsically good, or two men who held different opinions about the specific virtues essential to a good man, could be said to have different opinions about the proper ends of human action. They differ within a common framework of discussion, and therefore they agree at least in identifying and characterising the exact point of disagreement between them. The more philosophical disagreement is a difference of opinion about how opinions are properly to be formed and defended in this domain; therefore the two parties would not necessarily agree in identifying and characterising the exact point of divergence between them. There is no philosophically neutral description of the nature of their disagreement that both sides *must* accept as correct, beyond the acknowledged fact of disagreement itself. One philosopher may describe their difference as one of a *choice* of philosophies, the other may describe it as a difference of opinion. Both of them may be able to explain the appropriateness of their own descriptions within their own philosophies.

That disagreements about judgments of ultimate value, however these are expressed, are disagreements in opinion, and that they are most clearly expressed as disagreements about that which makes a man a good man, are both matters of opinion. Everyone who engages in moral and political argument can be driven to make judgments that are recognisable as judgments of ultimate value, in whatever form they are expressed. They are recognisable in his own behaviour as the judgments upon which he ultimately falls back when his political decisions and recommendations, his own more serious intentions and his more serious criticisms of men, are persistently questioned. In claiming that these judgments have the status of opinions, one may appeal to the fact that they are normally connected, in the habits of thought and speech of those who make them, with other statements, which would be quoted as supporting reasons, if the judgments were challenged. The force of the word 'opinion' is the implication that the demand for supporting reasons is always in place, and that there is an acknowledged commitment to doubt and reconsider the judgment if the supporting reasons are shown to be in themselves indefensible. But the philosophical thesis that judgments of value are to be interpreted as expressions of opinion is itself open to dispute as a matter of philosophical opinion. Within some philosophies, 'opinion' may be differently interpreted, as part of a systematic difference in the classification of judgments. The fact that the judgments are in fact normally supported by reasons, with the commitment to doubt and reconsider the judgments if the reasons are shown to be indefensible, may be held to be an insufficient reason for calling these judgments expressions of opinion. They may still be classified, within these philosophies, as decisions. There is no possibility of demonstrating, from some common and indisputable premises, that judgments of this kind *must* be called expressions of opinion. Considering them by themselves, and without appealing to some general, and therefore philosophical, classification of types of judgment, one can only point to the respects in which they resemble judgments that are generally called expressions of opinion, and to the fact that we do naturally speak of a man's philosophical, theological, moral, and political opinions, even when opinions of the utmost generality are intended. Whether the word 'opinion' or the word 'decision' is used, in either case there is the requirement of rationality; this is the requirement that the opinion or decision should be connected with other opinions and decisions in such a way that a doubt that undermines any one of them would also to a greater or less degree undermine the others. Perhaps this requirement of rationality really is universal; perhaps it is not a principle of a single philosophy, which may be rejected from some other vantage-point. Even those who, like G. E. Moore, have claimed to discriminate with final certainty, as if by the inner eye of the mind, that which is intrinsically good, have to justify their claim that certainty can be attained in this way. There is a theory of knowledge, exposed to the test of internal consistency, behind this claim.

The requirement of rationality, of connectedness of opinion, is universal, because judgments are made, and opinions are held, by men who, in proportion as they think at all, are necessarily trying to connect new judgments and opinions with those already formed. Within a single mind there is no alternative to this requirement of rationality except the abandonment of thought. When considering types of judgment as elements in language and in abstraction from individual minds, as in logic they must be considered, philosophers may underestimate the degree to which opinions are continually subject to revision in a single mind from many different directions. It is difficult to review all the possible rational grounds of a belief, and to hold in mind the whole system of its possible dependence upon other beliefs in every possible case. The opinions that form practical intentions and conduct, since they can always be formulated as opinions about human excellence, are the least easily studied and compared through the forms of their expression in words. They are often thoughts that are expressed mainly in practical intentions, and that are not communicated in words. Certainly they are opinions that *could* always be communicated, if the occasion arose, and they have their appropriate forms of expression. But the reasons that I may from time to time produce when communicating beliefs of this kind to others are often only a small selection, suitable to the occasion, from the grounds upon which the beliefs would be found to rest, if every connected belief was to be separately distinguished. They are not beliefs that men often need to put into words, except in very abstract and philosophical arguments and in the discussion of very general political principles. Their natural issue is in the intentions and decisions that guide action. One may have believed for many years that a certain specific activity was an essential human activity, and later have been convinced, by abstract argument and by personal experience, that it is comparatively trivial and inessential in the order of human virtues, and that it would be scarcely worth mentioning among the achievements of a man's life. This change of opinion may only have been expressed in a deliberate and self-conscious change in my own habits, a self-conscious re-direction of my interests. The change of opinion would lie behind the re-direction of my interests. If I were asked why I was no longer as interested as I had been in the activity in question, I would answer that I had changed my opinion about its place among the activities essential to men. I would then be implying that the change of interest was the outcome of reflection and that it had not happened without a self-conscious decision. In this case the change could equally well be described either as a change of opinion or as a change of intention. It would naturally be described rather as a change of opinion, when the reasons for the change have been deeply considered in advance and when they include changes of opinion about the truth of certain definite statements: definite statements, for example, that occur in a philosophical argument about the nature of freedom and intelligence.

That the thought which guides action may attain to different degrees of explicitness, and may correspond to different degrees of self-consciousness, has been a constant theme of this book. The more explicit a man is in formulating to himself the ends of his action, and the grounds upon which his decisions rest, the more he is aware of himself as having made choices between specific possibilities, choices that are always subject to revision. The more self-conscious he is in his criticism of his own intentions and activities, the more he is aware of the limits of his habits of classification, limits that determine the possibilities open to him. He becomes aware also of the limits set by the conventions of communication and classification into which he was born. He can begin endlessly to question and to criticise the vocabulary and the forms of language which he has learnt always to use in considering alternative ends of action. He cannot any longer consistently think of his more specific judgments of ultimate value as timeless truths, insulated from his practical intentions, or of his practical intentions at any time as disconnected from his opinions about the essential powers and interests of men. His moral and political opinions, and his practical intentions, are two phases of a single process of thought that always revolves in his mind around his idea of the activities that are essential to men as men, of those that are essentially destructive and that prevent men from realising their potentialities as human beings. One man differs from another in the degree of connectedness, and therefore of rationality, in his practical thinking. An irrational man does not pause to establish self-consciously in his own mind the exact order of dependence of his own opinions and intentions. He is not active in reviewing the whole range of his opinions and intentions, but rather passively finds them forming and changing without the deliberate imposition of an order on them. He is so much less free and less self-determining. Philosophical argument shows that the more specific methods of classification, both of types of conduct and of mental states, are relative to the prevailing practical interests and morality of a particular society. These philosophical arguments are only a generalisation of a truth recognised, at some lower level of generality, by every man who has ever regretted that he did not notice, because he had not been provided with the means to notice, some features of conduct or of states of mind now clearly entering into his intentions. No man therefore in his continuing thought about the activities essential to men can be satisfied to remain at a level of high abstraction, considering only such concepts as pleasure,

justice, friendship, intelligence and happiness. The growth
of civilised intelligence consists in always recognising and
discriminating new concrete forms and features of pleasure,
justice, friendship, intelligence and happiness. The history
of their discriminated forms at different phases of civilisation is the history of morality, and any individual can
similarly look back to the successive phases of discrimination in his own life. The type of moral philosophy that
considers only the use of the 'purely moral terms'—e.g.
'right', 'good', 'ought'—tends to be as vacuous and unin-
structive as the type of aesthetics that isolates the purely
aesthetic terms—e.g. 'beautiful'. A man's intentions must
at any one time be concentrated upon certain specific
forms of human achievement, and his choices are made
between these specific forms. There is no possibility of his
conduct being wholly controlled by any general theory,
which absolves him from making further discriminations
between different expressions of the essential virtues recognised in the theory. However firm and definite his opinions
about the order of human virtues and defects may be, he
must always in his practical reasoning look for an even
greater definiteness, and be open to the discovery of further
differences, requiring some further choice between more
specific alternatives. A general theory of the human virtues
and vices can only be the framework within which serious
practical reasoning is for a time concentrated. This framework is what remains of a man's opinions, now fixed and
definite, of the relative worth of human activities when he
reflects on the discriminations that he has already made.
He cannot avoid acknowledging, when he reflects, that
there are endlessly more discriminations to be made, even
within this same framework of general opinion.

Chapter 5

CONCLUSION

THE end of philosophy has been announced many times by modern philosophers. Speculation without the possibility of proof is superstition. The modern age does not need it. On the one side Hegel presented all previous philosophies as approximations to the final state of a fully civilised and self-conscious mind in a planned society. In the final form of society there would be no need for abstract speculation. Social institutions would be deliberately arranged to express every element of a developed human intelligence. Philosophy, in the form of abstract speculation, has a place only when there is a conflict between the ideals of pure reason and the misunderstood necessities of the actual forms of social life. In the perfect society, now coming into existence, the free man, assuming his self-imposed role in society, will express his freedom in his action as a citizen. He will no longer think of freedom as an abstract ideal, which always recedes in front of him. When the conflict disappears in the community of free, wise men, philosophy as abstract speculation will also disappear.

On the other side, empiricist philosophers have expected philosophy, in this scientific age, to be divided into mathematical logic and a more methodical study of the grammar and forms of common speech. They have claimed that their philosophy aims only to describe the misunderstood features of language as a working system of habits and conventions. Like Hegel, they have argued that philosophy in its ultimate phase should be purely descriptive, and not speculative. They differ from Hegel, first in confining their philosophical description to a single social institution, language, considered as a form of human behaviour; secondly, in describing the forms of language as they now exist, and not in the order of their development or in their perfect and final form. Both these prevailing schools of thought represent philosophical speculation as finally superseded. It is to be replaced either by the history of human thought up to its present and final phase, or by more exact factual and logical disciplines.

It has been the argument of this book that practical reasoning, if pressed to its conclusion, must always end in arguments that belong to the philosophy of mind. If this is true, disputable philosophical opinions are a necessary part of every phase of human thought. They arise directly from a man's critical reflections upon the reasoning that guides his own conduct, when he tries to choose for himself the terms in which the different possibilities of action open to him are to be identified and distinguished. This choice of the terms in which his intentions are to be formed is a condition of his regarding himself as a free and rational agent. It requires that he should have reviewed alternative methods of classifying conduct and its effects, and have found reasons for choosing one basis of classification rather than another. He needs to reflect on the concept of action itself, and to determine the sense in which a man can be said to be active in this thought, attitudes, states of mind, and feelings. There is no possibility of finding what is implied in having good grounds for actions and intentions unless the domain of action and intention is determined. There is no possibility of finding the notions of rationality and freedom clear, unless one has decided whether, and under what conditions, a man can be said to have reasons for his attitudes, desires, states of mind and feelings. The distinctions marked in current speech at his time and in his language are part of the evidence which he cannot ignore; they are necessarily for him his starting-point. But, like the concept of mind itself, they have a history, and they are changing. They cannot be left uncriticised, because other possibilities are always open.

That philosophical inquiry is interminable, and that it is necessary at every stage of thought, is a belief that rests on a set of contrasts that have occurred throughout the preceding argument. First, the contrast between the unlimited multiplicity of things and activities, and of features of things and activities, and our limited power to identify and distinguish them in a language. Secondly, the contrast between an individual's knowledge of his own situation, and of the causes that explain the limits of his own means of identifying the situation, and the intention to change his situation and to extend these limits. Thirdly, the contrast between a claim to universal validity in the grounds of our conduct, and of our criticism of ourselves, and the knowledge that the more specific grounds of conduct, and of the criticism of conduct, reflect a particular phase of social development, and a particular phase of the social institution of language. We know that our minds have been formed by the conventions of our present language and social institutions, and that we can only achieve a certain degree of detachment from them, even by the utmost efforts of reflection and comparison. As we at all times occupy a certain position in space and perceive everything from a certain point of view, so we occupy a certain position within the order of development of social institutions and think of men and of their potentialities

CONCLUSION

from this point of view. We know therefore that any philosophical inquiry into the conditions of freedom, and into the essential human virtues, will always need to be revised, however adequate it may seem to the particular conditions of its time, and to the concepts prevailing in the thought of that time. This philosophical inquiry, always resumed, is itself a necessary part of extending men's freedom of thought.

INDEX

Aesthetics, 119-20, 216-17, 220-1, 237, 244-7
Aristotle, 14, 147, 166, 167, 168, 212, 213, 232, 233, 258, 262

Belief, 100-1, 111, 124, 140-152, 155-60, 163-6, 264-9
Berkeley, 47, 49

Casuistry, 216-18
Classification, 12, 19-20, 35-38, 119, 209-10, 213-22, 224-36, 242-4, 267, 271
Cogito Ergo Sum, 73, 82
Colours, 35-6, 37, 122

Decision, 106-13, 116, 120, 125, 157-8, 171-6, 187, 190, 197, 240-1, 248, 264-9
Deliberation, 220, 224, 239-240, 248
Descartes, 73, 82-3, 87, 155, 233
Descriptions, Theory of, 201-204
Disposition, 164-5
Dreams, 64, 76, 79, 82-4, 94

Emotions, 199, 241, 243, 244
Existence, 25, 43, 73, 86-9, 204-5, 235

Feelings, 64-6, 91, 107, 122, 124-6, 241, 243, 244
Freedom, 133, 177-90, 209-210, 213-15, 222, 256, 271-3
Freud, 132, 133, 178, 191

Hegel, 233, 245, 270-1
Hume, 40, 45, 47, 51, 126, 233

Identification, 12-16, 20-1, 25-31, 35-6, 79, 85-9, 105, 121, 124, 146, 167, 192, 195-8, 210-12
Identity, 27, 28, 31, 35-8, 66, 75, 126, 205-6, 211, 223, 235, 239
Impressions, 26-30, 42-51, 56-9, 69, 71, 76
Individuation, 12-17, 35-8, 56-7

Kant, 13, 208, 222, 233, 245

Lawrence, D. H., 259
Linguistic Analysis, 233-5, 243, 253, 270-1
Locke, 48, 233

Memory, 72-3, 99, 255
Metaphysics, 237, 242-3
Moore, 260, 265

275